The Profit Motive in Education: Continuing the Revolution

The Profit Motive in Education: Continuing the Revolution

EDITED BY JAMES B. STANFIELD

The Institute of Economic Affairs

First published in Great Britain in 2012 by
The Institute of Economic Affairs
2 Lord North Street
Westminster
London SW1P 3LB
in association with Profile Books Ltd

The mission of the Institute of Economic Affairs is to improve public understanding of the fundamental institutions of a free society, with particular reference to the role of markets in solving economic and social problems.

A CIP catalogue record for this book is available from the British Library.

ISBN 978 0 255 36646 5
eISBN 978 0 255 36678 6

Typeset in Stone by MacGuru Ltd
info@macguru.org.uk

Printed and bound in Britain by Hobbs the Printers

CONTENTS

PART 2: LESSONS FROM THE UK AND ABROAD

THE AUTHORS

Daniel L. Bennett

Daniel L. Bennett is a Charles G. Koch Doctoral Fellow in Economics at Florida State University, a Research Fellow at the Center for College Affordability and Productivity, and a member of the Board of Advisors for *Career College Central* magazine. His research and writings related to higher education policy have been featured in media outlets such as *The New York Times, USA Today, Forbes, The Chronicle of Higher Education* and *Inside Higher Ed*.

Barbara Bergstrom

Barbara Bergstrom is a science teacher, and in 1993 she founded the Internationella Engelska Skolan (IES), which has since developed into a leading independent school group with 13,000 students enrolled in 18 secondary schools and one upper secondary school in Sweden. The company has an annual turnover of 1 billion krona (SEK), over 1,000 members of staff and is currently in a phase of rapid expansion. IES UK will be managing its first free school in Britain from autumn 2012. In 2009 Mrs Bergstrom received the 'Entrepreneur of the Year in Sweden' award.

Peje Emilsson

Peje Emilsson has had a long and successful career as a politician, entrepreneur and consultant in strategic communications. He founded Kunskapsskolan in 1999, having been active in the educational sector for a number of years. Today he is the Executive Chairman and majority shareholder of Kunskapsskolan Education. He is also the founder, Executive Chairman and largest shareholder of Kreab Gavin Anderson Worldwide, a leading advisory firm in financial, corporate and public affairs communications management serving clients in offices all over the world. Peje was Chef de Cabinet of the Paris-based International Chamber of Commerce from 1973 to 1981, and is today Chairman of the Stockholm Chamber of Commerce.

Frederick M. Hess

Frederick M. Hess is director of education policy studies at the American Enterprise Institute and is the author of many influential books on education, including *Education Unbound, Common Sense School Reform, Revolution at the Margins* and *Spinning Wheels*. Hess also serves as executive editor of *Education Next*, on the review board for the Broad Prize in Urban Education, and on the boards of directors of the National Association of Charter School Authorizers and the American Board for the Certification of Teaching Excellence. He holds an MA and PhD in Government from Harvard University as well as an MEd in Teaching and Curriculum.

Steven Horwitz

Steven Horwitz is the Charles A. Dana Professor of Economics at St Lawrence University in Canton, NY, and is also an Affiliated Senior Scholar at the Mercatus Center in Arlington, Virginia. He is the author of two books, *Microfoundations and Macroeconomics: An Austrian Perspective* (Routledge, 2000) and *Monetary Evolution, Free Banking, and Economic Order* (Westview Press, 1992), and he has written extensively on Austrian economics, Hayekian political economy, monetary theory and history, and the economics and social theory of gender and the family. Horwitz is the book review editor of the *Review of Austrian Economics* and a co-editor of the book series *Advances in Austrian Economics*.

Anders Hultin

Anders Hultin is an educational professional with two decades' experience of combining pioneering approaches to education with cutting-edge business thinking. Between 1991 and 1994 he worked as a political adviser to the Swedish Ministry of Schools and helped to introduce the voucher regime, which is now seen as a role model for countries around the world. In 1999 Anders co-founded Kunskapsskolan and was chief executive for eight years, during which time the company became the largest provider of secondary education in Scandinavia, operating thirty-two schools with more than ten thousand students. Anders was appointed chief executive of GEMS UK in August 2009, and in September 2010 he joined Pearson as their Managing Director of School Improvement in the UK.

Adam R. Lucchesi

Adam R. Lucchesi has taught economics at Ohio University and Bowling Green State University. He earned a Master's Degree in financial economics from Ohio University in 2007 and currently resides in the New York City metro area.

J. R. Shackleton

J. R. Shackleton is Professor of Economics at the University of Buckingham and an Economics Fellow at the IEA. Apart from his academic writings, he is a frequent commentator in the media. He has been Dean of two UK Business Schools, has worked in the Government Economic Service, and has lectured in many countries.

James B. Stanfield

James B. Stanfield is the development director at the E. G. West Centre, School of Education, Newcastle University. His research interests include: the history of private education prior to state intervention; the hidden costs and unintended consequences of government intervention in education; market-based solutions in education; the development of budget private schools in developing countries; and the development of inclusive business models in education. James writes a quarterly column on education for *Economic Affairs*, the journal of the IEA, and he is also a Fellow of the Adam Smith Institute.

Tom Vander Ark

Tom Vander Ark is managing partner of Learn Capital and

previously served as president of the X PRIZE Foundation and Executive Director of Education for the Bill & Melinda Gates Foundation, where he developed and implemented scholarship and grant programmes worth more than $3.5 billion to improve education throughout the United States. Tom is chairman of the International Association for K-12 Online Learning (iNACOL) and is a board director at several non-profits, including MLA Partner Schools and Strive for College. He also blogs at EdReformer.com.

Richard K. Vedder

Richard Vedder is the director of the Center for College Affordability and Productivity (CCAP) and studies higher education financing, labour economics, immigration, government fiscal policy and income inequality. A distinguished professor of economics at Ohio University, he is the author of several books, including *Going Broke by Degree* and *The Wal-Mart Revolution: How Big Box Stores Benefit Consumers, Workers, and the Economy* (with Wendell Cox). Dr Vedder earned his PhD in Economics from the University of Illinois.

Toby Young

Toby Young is the author of *How to Lose Friends and Alienate People* (2001) and *The Sound of No Hands Clapping* (2006). In addition to being a freelance journalist, he is the co-founder of the West London Free School, the first free school in England to sign a Funding Agreement with the Secretary of State for Education. To learn more about that project, visit the school's website on www.westlondonfreeschool.co.uk.

FOREWORD

In September 2011, Deputy Prime Minister Nick Clegg said:

> And, to anyone who is worried that, by expanding the mix of providers in our education system, we are inching towards inserting the profit motive into our school system, again, let me reassure you: yes to greater diversity; yes to more choice for parents; but no to running *schools* for profit, not in our state-funded education sector.[1]

This is an interesting position. No economic arguments were put forward to suggest that the profit motive would always give rise to poorer-quality results, so it is probably reasonable to assume that the deputy prime minister opposes the profit motive as a matter of principle. If so, why should that be? In general, the profit motive is not opposed in the provision of state-funded food or housing (for the less well off); in state-funded defence; in the provision of insurance; and, in most countries, in the provision of healthcare, whether state-funded or not. Indeed, many of the Christian democrat/social democrat countries of continental Europe do not preclude the profit motive in the provision of healthcare and some do not preclude it in the provision of education. In the UK and elsewhere, there are profit-making providers of nursery education – including state-funded providers – but,

1 The punctuation in this quotation has been changed.

apparently, as soon as children reach five years of age, the profit motive must be ruled out. Both the Labour Party when in government and David Willetts, the current minister for higher education, have suggested that the profit motive would be welcomed in higher education. There seems to be something specifically about education between the ages of five and seventeen that leads politicians to eschew profit-making institutions, but they are never explicit about the reasons.

Those who oppose the profit motive in all circumstances should state explicitly why they believe that profit will always lead to poorer-quality education. If they do not believe that the profit motive will always lead to poorer-quality education, presumably those who oppose the profit motive do so as a matter of principle. If so, they should be prepared to state explicitly what principle is at stake so that we can engage in proper debate. Presumably, if a politician is prepared to exclude the profit motive, even if it could be demonstrated that its adoption would lead to higher-quality education, the principle must be particularly compelling.

There is much empirical evidence on the benefits of education choice generally and on the benefits of the profit motive in particular. It is explicitly not the intention of this volume to summarise or further develop that body of evidence. Instead, the editor, James Stanfield, has put together a series of contributions that fulfil a number of important objectives in promoting a wider understanding of the need for the profit motive in education and how it has worked in practice in promoting innovation and a focus on good-quality education by entrepreneurs.

The first two chapters by Stanfield and Horwitz discuss basic principles. The benefits that the profit motive can bring in terms of signalling to providers that they are providing something of value in an efficient way are stressed. At the same time, both authors discuss the problem of the unforeseen consequences of government action. This will often come in the form of discrimination against private providers of education or the regulation of education in ways that distort incentives and can have perverse results. For Stanfield, the key value is freedom in education. Horwitz stresses that we should not be concerned about somebody's motives when they are providing good-quality education. In any case, just because a provider is not motivated by profit does not mean that they are not motivated by other forms of self-interest. Horwitz sums up as follows:

> ... the more important role of profits is to communicate knowledge about the efficiency of resource use and enable producers to learn what they are doing well or poorly ... what, in the absence of profits, will tell producers what they should and should not do[?] ... How will producers know not just what to produce but what inputs to use to produce it? ... Eliminating profit-seeking from an industry does not just require that a new incentive be found but that a new way of learning be developed as well. Profit is not just a 'motive', it is integral to the irreplaceable social learning process of the market. The very phrase 'the profit motive' reveals the critics' focus on motivation rather than the systemic communicative role played by profits and losses.

The second part of this monograph focuses on lessons from the UK and elsewhere. The lessons from the UK – see the chapter by Young – focus on the problems caused by the absence of the profit motive in the government's new 'free school' programme. There are real practical obstacles to setting up a free school, Young argues, that can only be overcome if profit-making firms are allowed to open free schools. If they are not, the programme might fail to deliver its potential. The chapters by Emilsson, Bergstrom and Stanfield show what can be achieved with a more liberal attitude – they also demonstrate how human nature is invariant in different economic and social conditions. Whether we are talking about developed countries such as Sweden or the poorest parts of India, profit-making schools can help transform education by ensuring that there is a relentless focus on the child's education and not on satisfying bureaucratic objectives. Margins are thin. Without that focus on the child's education, numbers attending such schools would fall and the profit margin could be eroded altogether. At the same time, the profit motive can promote what might be termed 'constructive and evolutionary' innovation and experimentation. New ideas can be tried and, if they succeed, they can be rapidly copied. In the non-profit sector, ideas are often copied less rapidly because the incentives are different and non-profit schools have less incentive – and less capital – to replicate and scale successful models. In the state sector, experimentation and innovation more often involve trying out new theories developed in education departments of universities on children whose parents cannot exercise a right of exit.

The chapter by Daniel L. Bennett, Adam R. Lucchesi and Richard K. Vedder first shows how the for-profit sector in US higher education has opened up opportunities for groups to which such opportunities had hitherto been closed. The facts are stark:

> More than half of students enrolled at for-profit institutions in 2007 were above 25 years of age, while only one quarter to one third of students attending private non-profit and public colleges were 25 years or older. Minorities also make up a larger share of for-profit enrolments than at public

> and private non-profit colleges, as black, Hispanic, Asian and American Indian students comprise nearly 40 per cent of total for-profit enrolments, whereas the same groups accounted for only 31 per cent and 25 per cent of enrolments in public and private non-profit institutions, respectively. Female students also account for a larger share of for-profit enrolments than at traditional institutions, making up 64 per cent of total for-profit enrolments: females accounted for 57 and 58 per cent of enrolment at public and private non-profit colleges, respectively.

Furthermore:

> For-profit students are also generally from lower socio-economic backgrounds than students at traditional colleges. According to an analysis by the Government Accountability Office, the annual median family income of for-profit students was 60 and 49 per cent of that of students attending public and private non-profit colleges, respectively, in 2004. They were also far more likely to be first-generation college students, as only 37 per cent of for-profit students reported having a parent with an associate's degree or higher, while 52 and 61 per cent of public and private non-profit students, respectively, reported the same. For-profit students are also likely to receive less family financial support, as 76 per cent were classified as financially dependent in 2007/08 versus 50 and 39 per cent of students in the public and private non-profit sectors, respectively.

Poorly designed regulation and government subsidy programmes, however, combined with free entry for profit-making organisations, can bring about some very undesirable consequences. The for-profit sector in the USA has, as a result, come under sustained political attack. It has some important advantages, but the implicit subsidies for failure within the US government system for financing higher education have distorted incentives and encouraged poor completion rates. The advantages the sector can bring may well outweigh the disadvantages substantially, but the government has been quick to capitalise on the problems. In the UK, the attack on for-profit higher education has even started before the sector has developed in any meaningful way. Furthermore, it seems that the UK government has not learned from US experience as our own student finance system is going to have significant cross-subsidies from taxpayers and those graduates who succeed to those who do not make best use of their qualifications. The authors of this chapter propose a level playing field between different types of higher education institutions but, at the same time, systems of government support that do not create perverse incentives within the for-profit sector. Higher education without a for-profit sector will be more exclusive and less flexible.

In the third section of the monograph the authors examine the potential for new models. Hultin asks why there is no IKEA in education. The profit motive should not be a threat, he argues, because: 'In a competitive environment profit reflects quality.' Hultin asks whether, if IKEA had set up as a charitable trust – perhaps to provide good-quality furniture to the less well off – it would ever have achieved the results it has achieved. Echoing Horwitz, it can be said that IKEA has been so successful at providing good-quality furniture to all – including those on limited means – because to do so is not its specific goal. Those foundations that specifically aim to provide education to people of limited means have little capacity or incentive to expand and replicate successful models and may not be as effective as organisations motivated by profit.

Shackleton argues that business schools should, in general,

operate more like businesses. There is room for the elite, academic schools but many are providing vocational skills and should be focusing on increasing the employability of graduates while widening their intake to provide more part-time education to those in the workforce. The profit motive, suggests Shackleton, will set these institutions free of the state and also set them free of the burden of cross-subsidising other parts of the universities to which they are attached. Government funding of teaching is already close to zero in this sector. As such, business schools would lose little financially while having much to gain in terms of greater freedom if they became profit-seeking corporations. Systems of government-guaranteed student finance might be appropriate for undergraduates, but some of the financial risk could be borne by the institutions themselves rather than by the taxpayer to ensure that you do not get the perverse incentives that exist in US higher education.

In his chapter, Hess argues that there is far too much emphasis put on school choice in political debate. Schooling represented the best practice for educating children a century ago. Simply giving parents a choice of schools is like giving people a choice between different telephones, ignoring the fact that innovation – driven by the profit motive – has led to the development of completely new ways of communicating. The objective should be good education, but education is a bundle of services which can be provided and combined in different ways. We need innovation and the profit motive to discover the best ways of combining different services in that bundle. Finally, Vander Ark explains how philanthropy can be combined with profit-making firms to scale new solutions in education, just as has happened in healthcare throughout the world. Vander Ark also expresses concern about the 'batch processing' of children that passes for education in much of the developed world and explains some of the innovations that are available. The irony is, of course, that children take to such innovation rather as a fish takes to water, but it is adult politicians who regulate the education sector in such a way that methods of providing education are largely rooted in the nineteenth century.

Overall, this is an important collection of work that makes a strong case that the pursuit of profit in the provision of education should be welcomed. The collection argues convincingly that to prohibit profit, or to prevent profit-making bodies receiving the same government funds as other bodies providing education, is to reject the most effective way of building a set of institutions that serves human needs in this field. The IEA thoroughly commends this volume to all who are interested in public policy in education.

The views expressed in this monograph are, as in all IEA publications, those of the authors and not those of the Institute (which has no corporate view), its managing trustees, Academic Advisory Council members or senior staff.

PHILIP BOOTH
Editorial and Programme Director,
Institute of Economic Affairs
Professor of Insurance and Risk Management,
Cass Business School, City University
April 2012

SUMMARY

- The criticism of the 'profit motive' in education is unjustified: we should not be concerned about the corporate structure of organisations that provide educational services. Furthermore, while people are disparaging about the profit motive they ignore other self-interested motives operating within the education sector, such as those within teachers' unions, government educational bureaucracies, and so on.
- The school reform debate currently focuses to too great an extent on 'school choice'. Instead, we need to focus on the supply side. By liberating the supply of education, we will see radical new ways to deliver education, including new ways of bundling education services. Those models that are successful will be scaled up rapidly if the profit motive is allowed to work.
- The UK government is wrong to exclude profit-making schools from its free-school programme and it might fail as a result. Allowing profit-making free schools would draw more capital into the sector; allow people who wished to take financial risks to do so while reducing risks for parents and other groups involved in setting up free schools; help ensure that the necessary site and buildings can be obtained and financed; and radically reduce the cost of regulation.
- Non-profit foundations generally do not have the ability or

incentives to scale up successful practices and roll them out widely. They are therefore not the answer to promoting high-quality education available to all.

- Profit-making schools in Sweden have raised standards and provided a competitive spur to state schools. One chain of schools has increased teacher contact time by 50 per cent through developing curriculum materials that can easily be adapted by teachers.
- The UK lags behind the UN in terms of developing good practice in education policy – despite the fact that the UN tends to lag behind best practice by many years itself. The UN has taken an empirical approach and has decided that, if profit-making schools can raise educational standards, they should be welcomed. If the UN's success is to be spread more widely so that the profit motive is accepted by national governments in developed countries, those supporting the profit motive must choose their language prudently. Words such as 'inclusive', 'diverse' and 'open' can be applied to an education sector that is not limited to state institutions and can be helpful in winning the political debate.
- For-profit higher education institutions in the USA have opened up universities and colleges to groups in society that have previously been excluded. More than half of students at for-profit institutions in 2007 were over 25 years old and ethnic minority enrolments comprised nearly 40 per cent of the total. Furthermore, a greater proportion of students at for-profit institutions were 'first generation' students whose parents did not have a degree.
- There are, however, important lessons from the USA for UK policy. Mechanisms of government financing can

distort incentives and lead to lower completion rates than is desirable. The UK government seems to be repeating the mistakes made in the USA by directing greater subsidies towards those former students who do not make best use of their degree courses. The advantages of profit-making institutions should not be forgotten, however, and it would be better to correct the distorting systems of government financing than to undermine the for-profit sector.

- UK business schools are not entirely the success story that is often claimed. Graduate unemployment from UK business schools is higher than the average for all graduates. Reform is needed. Business schools operating in the 'mass market' for business education should be profit-making. This would bring stronger customer focus, cost control, expertise from other service areas, links with other businesses and new sources of capital.
- In general, private capital and the profit motive are needed to create widely replicated, low-margin, low-cost methods of education. Such innovation will lead to the development of entirely new personal learning formats and services and move the sector away from the 'batch processing' of children in classrooms where children of the same age progress through material at the same pace.

TABLES AND FIGURES

PART 1: BASIC CONCEPTS

1 INTRODUCTION

James B. Stanfield

Ah, you miserable creatures! You who think that you are so great! You who judge humanity to be so small! (Bastiat, 2002: 67)

Questioning the anti-profit mentality

Recent research carried out in the USA has found that the American public often associate greater levels of profit with social harm and for-profit organisations are often viewed as less socially valuable than non-profit organisations. Profits were also seen as coming from a fixed pie and so increasing profits for one person could be achieved only by decreasing profits for somebody else. The authors of this research therefore concluded that 'even in one of the most market-oriented cultures in the world, people doubt the ability of profit-seeking business to benefit society' (see Bhattacharjee et al., 2011: 4).

This negative perception of the profit motive is not a new or recent development (see Hayek, 1988: ch. 6). In 1948, the US economist Henry Hazlitt stated that '[t]he indignation shown by many people today at the mention of the very word profits indicates how little understanding there is of the vital function that profits play in our economy' (Hazlitt, 1948: 5). Six years later Joseph Schumpeter also commented on the fact that people seem to exhibit an 'ineradicable prejudice that every action intended to serve the profit interest must be anti-social by this fact alone' (Schumpeter, 1954: 234).

Fast-forward to the present day and the concept of profit still remains one of the most misconceived subjects in economics, and this applies to an even greater extent in the field of education. Consider, for example, the following headline from an editorial in the *Observer* newspaper: 'Educating children should not be for profit – Learning has always been separate from the forces of the free market. And that's how it should stay' (4 April 2010). According to the *Observer* the issue appears to be black and white. The profit motive and learning simply do not mix, they never have and they never will. The debate is therefore closed. This statement raises more questions than it answers, however.

Firstly, would the *Observer* still be prepared to support its claim that 'educating children should not be for profit' if schools run by for-profit companies could be shown to produce much better results at a lower cost – especially for the less well off? Or should these schools be permanently precluded irrespective of how they perform? While the *Observer* – and many politicians – might claim that no such evidence exists, we should also question why they are not interested in finding out which type of school performs the best. Are they confident in their belief that all government schools will always outperform all schools run by for-profit companies, both now and at any time in the future? Or is there some objection in principle to the profit motive, even if the education of children suffers as a result of excluding it?

Secondly, the burden of proof must surely be placed on those who want to maintain the current restrictions on parents and the resulting government monopoly. Even if some parents would choose an inferior school rather than a superior one that was profit-making, is the *Observer* suggesting that parents who see the matter differently should not be able to choose a profit-making school? Is the profit motive so obnoxious that it should not be allowed to prevail for those whose priority is simply a high-quality education? And why are parents deemed to be capable of voting politicians into power, but then deemed incapable of choosing the best school for their children? If parents are deemed to be ignorant, then why not extend this argument to its logical conclusion and demand that their right to vote should also be removed?

Thirdly, how can the *Observer* justify campaigning so passionately for freedom and a free market within the press and the media, while at the same time campaigning for the restriction of freedom and almost total government control over children's schooling? How can freedom and a free market be so fundamentally important when it comes to the market for newspapers or children's books, but dismissed when applied to children's schooling? And why is political control, central planning and a government monopoly deemed to be unacceptable within the media but welcomed in education?

In the above quotation the *Observer* then goes on to proudly state that 'learning has always been separate from the forces of the free market'. This statement shows how confused this debate has now become. For example, if the forces of the free market include the freedom of parents to choose and the freedom of private providers to enter the sector, then this suggests that the *Observer* believes and indeed celebrates the idea that learning has always been separate from these forces of freedom. But if freedom refers to choice, autonomy, self-determination, independence, openness and the lack of restrictions, then how can restricting these forces be a good thing? And if learning has always been separate from these forces, what other superior forces have been at play? After all, what could possibly be more important than the forces of freedom in education?

There is also a mountain of historical evidence that clearly shows how a wide range of forms of learning emerged spontaneously with the help of religious, charitable and private providers. This has included profit-making schools. But when we define education more widely, the profit motive has often been at work, in the growth and development of the printing press, libraries (see Stanfield, 2010), schools, colleges and even newspapers.[1]

If the *Observer* were referring only to the development of children's schooling during the twentieth century then its argument would certainly hold more weight. For the way in which successive governments have protected government schools with subsidies and excluded and discriminated against all other schools has gradually crowded out a variety of private providers and transformed the sector from one which was open and competitive to one which is now closed and dominated by one monopoly provider.

Despite this transformation of education from the private to the public sector, the profit motive has continued to play an important role behind the scenes. For example, every school building, every table and chair, every textbook and computer and every pen, pencil and piece of paper used in government schools is purchased on the market from companies driven by the profit motive. For-profit companies also currently dominate the provision of state-funded nursery schooling, which suggests that

1 Indeed, newspapers promote learning and the *Observer* is currently owned by a for-profit company. It was established in 1791 by W. S. Bourne on the simple premise that 'the establishment of a Sunday newspaper would obtain him a rapid fortune'.

the government trusts these companies to provide schooling to children up to age five, but not beyond. As this policy now dictates the nature and form of nursery schooling across the country, politicians must explain why the profit motive works for the youngest children but not for those aged six and above.

There are also hundreds of for-profit companies, such as the Early Learning Centre (ELC), which sell a variety of different learning products and services directly to parents to help engage children in the process of learning. When learning materials are purchased from ELC, I doubt that parents will be concerned with the legal status of ELC or with what motivates the company to sell learning games and materials. Instead a simple transaction takes place in which both parties are expected to profit – a genuine win-win situation. If the profit motive plays such an important role in helping companies such as ELC to develop and expand to help meet the learning needs of parents and children, why would the same also not apply if ELC decided to open and manage a school? In fact wouldn't trusted brands such as ELC be particularly well placed to expand into schooling if given the opportunity?

Finally, outside the government monopoly, there are a number of schools that are owned and managed by for-profit companies which continue to exist, without receiving any government subsidies. For example, in December 2010 there were 489 mainstream proprietorial schools in England, educating 82,528 children (see Croft, 2010). The continued existence of these schools and the wider role of the profit motive in education suggest that there is not a fundamental conflict between the two. If there were then parents would have deserted these schools a long time ago, forcing them either to transform how they operate or to go out of business. And if these schools have managed to survive in such a difficult working environment (where they have to compete with a free government alternative and where all of their potential customers have already been forced to pay for government schooling through taxation), then perhaps they have the potential to play a much greater role if given the opportunity to compete on a level playing field. The existence of these schools highlights yet another inconsistency in this debate. When parents pay for their children's education themselves they are free to invest in private schooling. When the government attempts to spend parents' money on their behalf, however, private schooling is no longer viewed as an acceptable option.

It is simply not true that learning has been completely separate from the forces of the free market and the profit motive. What is true is that the government has a particular blind spot about combining the profit motive with government-financed schooling for those aged between five and seventeen and that, with regard to university education, liberalisation has come only very recently and tentatively. It is unfortunate, however, that this blind spot exists in the sector that provides schooling that largely determines the quality of education and life chances of most of the population.

Things seen and not seen in education

As previously noted by Bastiat, the task of examining public policy is complicated by the fact that government interventions can often produce not just one immediate and visible effect (what is seen), but a series of hidden effects and unintended consequences which emerge over time (what is not seen). It is important to recognise the difference between the two because, while the immediate effects of a policy may be favourable, the long-term consequences can sometimes be disastrous. Bastiat therefore makes an important distinction between the bad economist, who considers only what is seen, and the good economist, who is also prepared to take into account what is not seen.

Writing approximately one hundred years later, Henry Hazlitt also suggested that the art of economics consists in 'looking not merely at the immediate but at the longer effects of any act or policy; it consists in tracing the consequences of that policy not merely for one group but for all groups' (Hazlitt, 1948: 5). Furthermore, according to Hazlitt, the most frequent fallacy in economics is the idea that one should concentrate on the short-run effects of policies on special groups and ignore the long-run effects on the community as whole.

Unfortunately, it is difficult to escape the fact that the history of government intervention in education in the UK has been dominated by this fallacy and as a result the sector continues to suffer from the long-run consequences of ill-thought-out policies from the remote past. The current practice of subsidising only government schools while discriminating against all private alternatives provides a good example of a policy based almost entirely on what is seen, while neglecting what is not seen.

Firstly, it is important to note that government subsidies were initially introduced to help fill in the gaps in an already flourishing private sector. Subsidies were therefore meant to follow children from low-income families to an existing private school or a new government school, depending upon parents' preferences. The suggestion that these parents should now be penalised and have the ability to choose removed simply because they were poor and in receipt of subsidies was deemed to be unfair and unacceptable.

Secondly, at a later date, the change in policy was driven by the rent-seeking activities of local authorities and had nothing to do with the needs of parents and children. Local authorities simply preferred to spend the money that they had raised in taxes on their own schools instead of sharing it with existing private schools. The reason why government schools should receive preferential treatment and why all private providers should be discriminated against was never explicitly justified. In many senses, it happened by accident.

Thirdly, while those who previously introduced and championed these policies focused their attention on what was seen – the immediate and visible benefit of opening a new free government school – they clearly failed to take into account what was not seen – the long-term impact on local private schools, which would increasingly find it difficult to compete with a free alternative and would eventually be crowded out of the market altogether. The unintended result was the growth of a government monopoly in the provision of schooling with government schools simply replacing the majority of private schools.[2]

Fourthly, as each new government now inherits a national network of government schools, a 'national plan' is now 'required' and politicians are drawn into making increasingly detailed decisions concerning almost every aspect of children's schooling. Over time the needs and demands of parents are gradually sidelined

2 The schooling of children therefore represents the only service sector which has been nationalised almost by accident. It has certainly not been the product of enlightened government planning – which perhaps helps to explain why the denationalisation of education is proving to be so difficult. As no one really knows or understands why schooling was nationalised in the first place, it is proving to be much more difficult to justify why this approach has failed and why denationalisation is now required.

and replaced by the views and opinions of politicians and their policy experts. The government now begins to dictate what is meant by quality in education and parents are simply forced to accept what the government provides.

As the government monopoly develops it soon becomes clear that those who were originally supposed to benefit from government subsidies (i.e. those from low-income families) are now the ones who gain the least from the current system. While middle-income and high-income families may choose to send their child to a good private school or move to an area where good government schools are located, low-income families remain trapped in areas where many failing government schools still exist.

Finally, as the government now controls education, this provides an army of regulators, politicians and other vested interests with a free rein to use education to try to achieve a variety of social goals, such as decreasing inequality or improving social cohesion. High-achieving children now become teaching tools to help improve the education of low-achieving children and all children from different backgrounds are now forced to attend the same school to ensure that they all get exactly the same kind and level of education. According to Bastiat, the natural tendency of the human race towards liberty is thwarted because of this very kind of activity – the fatal desire of politicians to 'set themselves above mankind in order to arrange, organise and regulate it according to their fancy' (Bastiat, 2002: 67).

The ultimate charge, therefore, against the current government restrictions on education and the resulting government monopoly is not only that it has systematically failed to deliver an acceptable standard of education to all children irrespective of income and location, but that it has also restricted and undermined freedom in education. This includes the freedom of parents to choose the nature and form of education which their children receive and also the freedom to choose the institution from which their children receive education. In fact government attempts to restrict these freedoms in education have been the key problem facing the sector for over one hundred years. The current method of subsidising education can therefore be viewed as a simple form of protectionism, whereby government subsidies are used to protect government schools from all private sector alternatives from both home and abroad with the losers from the protectionism being the least well off. The government therefore finds itself in the perverse situation of attempting to improve education by severely restricting the kind of organisations that are allowed to provide it.

Policy lessons

So far, we have provided the political backdrop against which education policy operates. Policy is dictated not just by vested interests within government but also by an intellectual elite that is hostile to the profit motive, innovation and entrepreneurialism in education. In the remainder of this chapter, we examine some broad and specific policy proposals that can help get education policy back on track and then finish with a more radical vision for the future.

There is no conflict between the profit motive and education

Evidence from history and the present day, from both home and abroad, clearly shows that there is no conflict between the profit motive and the provision of good-quality learning and education of all forms. If we reduce education to a simple act of voluntary exchange, then it is clear that it is very similar to the vast majority of other products and services that are traded freely on an open market. In short, both parties profit. On the one hand, parents profit from being able to provide education for their children that they could not provide themselves. On the other hand, the for-profit provider will profit as long as the revenue received is greater than the costs incurred. It is also clear that those children who receive the education will be expected to profit from the experience. And, finally, the wider community will profit in the long run from this act of voluntary exchange as there are benefits from a better-educated community with higher rates of employment and a greater understanding of history, science and culture.

It is also clear that for-profit companies operate very differently from their non-profit counterparts and have a lot to offer the world of education. The profit motive acts as an incentive to continually keep costs down and to continually look for more efficient ways of operating. Furthermore, profit acts as a signal that the provider is being successful in these respects. Secondly, for-profit companies have access to private finance from both home and abroad which will allow them to expand their model of education if it proves to be successful. The profit motive also encourages specialisation – a process which appears to have completely bypassed much of the education sector to date. Therefore, instead of attempting to be all things to all persons, schools of the future may increasingly begin to buy in specialist providers that can provide a much better service at a lower cost than if the school attempted to deliver the same services itself. This can include the provision of curricula materials or, perhaps, the use of local sports clubs and professionals for physical education. The profit signals will indicate whether such specialisation is fruitful. The profit motive can provide the incentives for a school to attract and retain talented teachers by deviating from bureaucratically determined pay rates.

Perhaps more importantly, with effects that are very difficult to predict in advance, the profit motive will help attract a new generation of educational entrepreneurs who are prepared to think the unthinkable and blaze new trails in education. Those that succeed will prosper and be copied; those that fail will fade away. Part of entrepreneurship is the process of research, development and continual innovation at the local level as each education company seeks to discover more efficient and effective methods, models and approaches.

Freedom in education is the key ingredient

While the profit motive is essential in ensuring that we have a thriving education sector, it is not sufficient to guarantee the best education possible. This is because the profit motive may also encourage some companies to seek government protection against all forms of competition, resulting in a private monopoly, which brings with it many of the problems associated with a public monopoly. The key question therefore is not whether for-profit companies should be free to deliver publicly funded education, but whether there should be freedom of entry to all different types of organisation from both home and abroad. Furthermore, parents must also be free to choose between a variety of private alternatives and the government should not restrict that freedom except *in extremis.*

There is no one best model of a school, college or university

In education markets around the world where government restrictions have been removed, it is becoming increasingly clear that there is no single best model of a school, college or university. Instead there are a variety of different legal and organisational forms and structures active in this sector, which, in turn, adopt a variety of different financial, management and educational models and practices to help them deliver a variety of different educational opportunities. We should also expect different models, structures and forms to emerge as markets develop and the rate of innovation begins to increase.

If developing countries can, why can't we?

To date UK governments have looked to the USA and to Europe for much-needed inspiration on how to break the government monopoly in education. There are now, however, an increasing number of developing countries that are much more open, enthusiastic and willing to embrace and encourage the role of the private sector in education. As a result, inspiration for future reforms is likely to come from the developing world.

Four simple policy proposals

End all discrimination against private providers

All different types of public, private and charitable organisations should have an equal opportunity to deliver publicly funded education. Therefore, when the government is distributing public funds in education, it must end all discrimination against all private providers. An *inclusive* education policy should be adopted which does not exclude any type of provider. After this principle has been established, public funds can then be redirected towards parents who will then be free to choose between a variety of different providers.

Abolish all corporation and capital gains tax on for-profit education companies

To encourage private investment in education the government should abolish all corporation and capital gains tax on all for-profit education companies. As it stands, all schools run by private non-profit organisations are exempt from paying all forms of corporation and capital gains tax. This stands in stark contrast to schools managed by for-profit companies, which must pay corporation and capital gains tax, thereby placing them at a relative disadvantage to their non-profit rivals. While these two different legal structures used not to compete in the same market, they are beginning to do so. Therefore, to help create a level playing field in education and to encourage the growth of the for-profit private sector, tax-exempt status should be available to both for-profit and non-profit organisations. For the government the important point is not whether the entrepreneur acts out of altruistic or selfish motives, but whether his actions benefit society or not. Educational entrepreneurs would then be free to choose among a number of organisational forms on the basis of their efficiency and not on the basis of their tax advantages. This would mean that any entrepreneur who sets up a private school would receive preferential tax treatment. The tax subsidy would therefore not depend on the corporate form of the organisation but would be granted to all providers of education because of their perceived social value. This levelling of the playing field should also apply to higher education and to value added tax (from which charitable organisations are exempt).

Inform parents of the annual cost of their children's education

Despite everybody preaching about the importance of education and the need for parents to be better informed, it still remains the case that parents across the country have very little, if any, idea about how much money is being invested by central and local government in their children's education. As most parents will be paying for their children's education through taxation, the government clearly has a responsibility to provide this information annually to each parent. On the one hand, this will help parents make better-informed decisions on whether they are getting value for money from their existing government school. On the other hand, it will also provide potential private providers with important information concerning the current costs of government schooling in different locations across the country.

An association of private providers

To date, existing (and potential future) private providers of education have failed to explain to politicians and the public how they could help to transform education if only they were given the opportunity to do so. An association of private providers is required to help the private sector present a unified voice. It is also clear that, owing to the sensitive nature of education, both politicians and the public are going to want a number of safeguards in place that will protect children's education from business failure, financial mismanagement and bankruptcy. Therefore, instead of looking to the government to find a solution, an association of private providers could begin to address this issue itself and present the government with a number of preferred solutions. Other key concerns relating to the content of the curriculum and basic issues of quality control could also be addressed by an association, to help ensure that all its members conform to a general set of guidelines (see Stanfield, 2005).

The primary purpose of the new association will be to bring education companies together to participate in the promotion of private sector interests within the policymaking process. Market-based reforms will have to be sold in the political marketplace and their success may well depend on how they are presented and communicated to the appropriate audience. The publication of an annual report will allow the association to survey its members on a regular basis to find out how existing laws and regulations are affecting their ability to compete and increase investment. Together with representing education companies within the policymaking process, a future association will also have to work hard at redressing decades of discrimination against private education within the media and especially within the trade union movement. Once an association is established, opportunities may also arise for education companies to collaborate on a variety of issues, including joint research projects, private teacher training courses and private alternatives to the existing qualifications framework. Organising an annual national conference will also help to raise the profile of the association and its members within the media and investment community, and will allow members to discuss and debate issues of mutual interest.

A vision of the liberal ideal of education

To date, many of the arguments put forward in favour of allowing for-profit companies to set up and manage state-funded schools have focused on a number of practical arguments, such as the need to improve the performance of failing government schools, the need for additional school places and the general desire to ensure that all children can benefit from the best schools available, irrespective of income or location. This arises from the 'what matters is what works' school of politics, where ideological principles are no longer relevant.

While this evidence-, results- or outcomes-based approach can be very persuasive, it may not be sufficient if the proposed reforms are to win widespread support among both politicians and the general public. According to Nobel laureate James Buchanan, evidence of 'what works' must be supplemented by a vision of the liberal ideal that attempts to capture the minds of people (see Buchanan, 2000).

Consider, for example, the suffragettes who were campaigning for the right to vote at the start of the twentieth century. Their case for reform was not based on any evidence which showed that extending the right to vote to women would guarantee a better election result than the existing voting system. In fact, many opponents of the reforms (mostly men, but not exclusively) warned of the perverse consequences and the chaos that would follow if women were allowed to vote on the important and complicated matters of national government. Instead the suffragette movement was campaigning for a fundamental freedom and a basic human right – the freedom and right of women to vote. A voting system based upon universal franchise was therefore deemed to be superior to one based upon a restricted franchise, irrespective of the results or outcomes of subsequent elections. In this example the evidence-based approach was clearly of limited use and, in fact, it could be argued that those who attempted to appeal to evidence had completely misunderstood the nature of the problem and the key issues at stake.

This same line of reasoning could also be applied to the current debate in education. An education system in which all parents have the freedom to choose would be deemed to be superior to the current system, which continues to restrict these freedoms. Any appeal to evidence or what works would therefore be dismissed as irrelevant. Buchanan refers to the repeal of the Corn Laws in the nineteenth century as a successful example of when evidence was supplemented by a vision of the liberal ideal to help gain support for proposed reforms. If we are to heed his advice, then a national campaign for the repeal of laws restricting freedom in education is now required. This presents the exciting prospect of an education system in which all parents are free to choose.

A campaign for freedom in education would be based on the principle that it is parents and not politicians who are ultimately responsible for their children's education – a responsibility which can only be carried out if parents are free to choose the nature, form and content of education which their children receive. Parental choice or freedom in education therefore is not desirable simply because it may help to improve the efficiency of failing government schools. Nor is parental choice in education simply the latest policy reform that will go out of fashion in a few years' time. Instead, it is important for the same reasons that religious freedom or freedom of the press is important – because they are both recognised as basic human rights or fundamental freedoms, which deserve to be respected and protected at all costs.

A vision of the liberal ideal in education would therefore recognise that the responsibility for educating children cannot be transferred to others; nor can it be sidelined or placed behind other considerations. Instead, it is the key principle upon which the whole education system is based. This means that governments must not in any way restrict, undermine or distort this important relationship between parent and child and the natural growth and development of education. As a result, it will not be the role of politicians to dictate which schools children should or should not attend or how much parents should invest in their children's education. This will, once again, be the responsibility of parents. Nor will it be the role of politicians to dictate who can and cannot set up and manage a school. The liberty to teach and the freedom to educate must be respected, and it will ultimately be parents who decide whether a new school will flourish or not.

While politicians have previously argued that education is far too important to be left to ignorant parents and the chaos of the market, they must now be prepared to admit that education is far too important to be left to politicians. Politicians must have the humility to recognise that their own personal views on education are irrelevant. After all, what does any politician know about the detailed and very specific circumstances of each and every pupil and parent across the UK?

Therefore, a future education sector where the rights and responsibilities of parents are both respected and protected will not be planned or directed by central government, nor will it be used to achieve any 'national' objectives. Instead, it will consist of a variety of different national and international private, independent, autonomous, for-profit and not-for-profit institutions, each with its own specific mission. The needs and desires of parents (and not politicians or governments) will be supreme, and the government will be restricted to establishing a regulatory framework that will encourage a variety of different institutions to compete and flourish on a level playing field.

According to Buchanan a vision of the liberal ideal would also be based upon our desire to be free from the coercive power of others, combined with the absence of a desire to exert power over others. Another Nobel laureate, Milton Friedman, explains further:

> Willingness to permit free speech to people with whom one agrees is hardly evidence of devotion to the principle of free speech; the relevant test is willingness to permit free speech to people with whom one thoroughly disagrees. Similarly, the relevant test of the belief in individual freedom is the willingness to oppose state intervention even when it is designed to prevent individual activity of a kind one thoroughly dislikes. (Friedman, 1962)

Therefore, this provides a useful test for all those 'miserable creatures' who continue to view schools run by for-profit companies as an unnecessary – or perhaps a necessary – evil. Do they have the discipline to place their personal views to one side and recognise that the rights and responsibilities of individual parents must always come first? If they do, then they should be willing to oppose the existing government restrictions which prevent profit-making companies from managing state-funded schools, despite the fact that they may not want their children to attend such a school. From this perspective, a vision of the liberal ideal should be seen as much less self-obsessed and instead much more compassionate towards the private beliefs and the opinions of those who are directly responsible for children's education – their parents.

For those politicians concerned with the 'vote motive', the fact that all parents are also voters might imply that reforms that increase parents' freedom to choose in education have a good chance of gaining electoral support if the case for reform is communicated and presented in the correct way. The time may also be right to launch a campaign for freedom in education, because a vision which is based upon liberty and democracy is currently a common denominator of both the Conservative and Liberal Democratic parties. There can be nothing more liberal and democratic than extending the right to choose to all parents, irrespective of their income or location. The following advice from Bastiat should therefore appeal to both parties:

> Away, then, with quacks and organizers! Away with their rings, chains, hooks, and pincers! Away with their artificial systems! Away with the whims of governmental administrators, their socialized projects, their centralization, their tariffs, their government schools, their state religions, their free credit, their bank monopolies, their regulations, their restrictions, their equalization by taxation, and their pious moralizations!
>
> And now that the legislators and do-gooders have so futilely inflicted so many systems upon society, may they finally end where they should have begun: May they reject all systems, and try liberty. (Bastiat, 2002: 85)

References

Bastiat, F. (2002), *The Law*, London: Institute of Economic Affairs.

Bhattacharjee, A., J. Dana and J. Baron (2011), *Is Profit Evil?*

Associations of Profit with Social Harm, Philadelphia: University of Pennsylvania.

Buchanan, J. M. (2000), 'The soul of classical liberalism', *Independent Review*, V(1): 111–19.

Croft, J. (2010), *Profit-making Free Schools – Unlocking the Potential of England's Proprietorial Schools Sector*, London: Adam Smith Institute.

Friedman, M. (1962), *Capitalism and Freedom*, Chicago, IL: University of Chicago Press.

Hayek, F. A. (1988), *The Fatal Conceit: The Errors of Socialism*, London: Routledge.

Hazlitt, H. (1948), *Economics in One Lesson*, New York: Harper.

Schumpeter, J. (1954), *History of Economic Analysis*, New York: Oxford University Press.

Stanfield, J. (2005), 'An association for UK education businesses', *Economic Affairs*, 25(3): 75–6.

Stanfield, J. (2010), 'The rise and fall of for-profit libraries', *Economic Affairs*, 30(3): 95.

2 PROFIT IS ABOUT LEARNING, NOT JUST MOTIVATION

Steven Horwitz

One of the more common complaints from critics of the market is that the profit motive works in opposition to people and firms doing 'the right thing'. We hear this complaint made about a number of industries, from healthcare to the law to the one that will concern us here: education. The argument is often made that one of the advantages of government-provided education is that our children are not at the mercy of the profit motive in determining who will educate them and how. Implicit in this complaint is that if the education market were, in fact, based more on profit and loss, somehow education would suffer. An additional implication is that we have tried providing education via the profit-and-loss process of the market and that somehow this failed, leading us to substitute government provision for the cold calculation of profit.

The critics seem to suggest that, if people and firms were motivated by something besides profit, they would be (or perhaps are) better able to provide the things that people really need. The sorry record of government-provided education would suggest otherwise, but to understand fully why the state has failed so miserably, we need to take a deeper look at the role that profit and loss plays in a market economy.

The distinction between intentions and results

The first thing to note is that the critics are blaming a 'motive' for the problems they supposedly see. The overarching problem with blaming a 'motive' is that it ignores the distinction between intentions and results. That is, it ignores the possibility of unintended consequences, both beneficial and harmful. Since Adam Smith, economists have understood that self-interest (of which the profit motive is just one example) of producers can lead to social benefits. As Smith famously put it, it is not the 'benevolence' of the baker, butcher and brewer which leads them to provide us with our dinner but their 'self-love'. Smith's insight, which was a core idea of the broader Scottish Enlightenment of which he was a part, puts the focus on the consequences of human action, not what motivates it. What we care about is whether the goods get delivered, not the motivation of those who provide it. Smith led economists to think about why it is, or under what circumstances, self-interest will lead to beneficial unintended consequences. It is perhaps human nature to assume that intentions equal results, or that self-interest means an absence of social benefit. Perhaps in the small, simple societies in which humanity evolved that was often the case. In the more complex, anonymous world of what F. A. Hayek called 'the Great Society', however, the simple equation of intentions and results does not hold.

As Smith recognised, what determine whether the search for profit leads to good results are the institutions through which human action is mediated. Institutions, laws and policies affect which activities are profitable and which are not. Our intentions are mediated through these institutions in order to produce results. A good economic system is one in which those institutions, laws and policies are such that the self-interested behaviour of producers leads to socially beneficial outcomes.

In mixed economies like that of the USA, it is often the case that the institutional framework rewards profit-seeking behaviour that does not produce social benefit, or, conversely, prevents profit-seeking behaviour that could produce such benefits. For example, if agricultural policy pays farmers not to grow food, then the profit motive will lead to lower food supplies. If environmental policy confiscates land with endangered species on it, owners of such land who are driven by the profit motive will 'shoot, shovel and shut up' (i.e. kill off and bury any endangered species they find on their land). If banking policy subsidises risky lending, banks will be more likely to make bad loans. And if energy policy subsidises, or limits the liability of, nuclear power plants, we will be more likely to see them creating problems.

Ignoring the difficult questions

Before blaming the profit motive for the problems in an industry, critics might want to look at the ways in which existing government programmes might lead firms and professionals to engage in behaviour that is profitable but does not benefit consumers. Labelling the profit motive as the source of the problem enables the critics to ignore the really difficult questions about how institutions, policies and laws affect the profit-seeking incentives of producers and how that profit-seeking behaviour translates into outcomes. Placing the blame on the profit motive without qualification simply overlooks the Smithian question of whether or not better institutions would enable the profit motive to generate better results and whether current policies or regulations are the source of the problem because they guide the profit motive in ways that produce the very problems the critics identify.

For example, the high cost of private education in the USA might be the result of a whole variety of regulations placed on private primary and secondary schools, as well as the lack of competition resulting from these high barriers to entry (and the difficulty of competing with taxpayer-supported government schools). Ignoring the way institutions might affect what is profitable is often due to a more general blind spot about the possibility of self-interested behaviour generating unintended beneficial consequences. Before we attempt to banish the profit motive, should we not attempt to see whether we can make it work better?

Placing blame for social problems on the profit motive is also easy if such critics do not offer an alternative. What should be the basis for determining how resources are allocated if not in terms of profit-seeking behaviour under the right set of institutions? How should people be motivated, if not by profit? Often this question is just ignored, as critics are just interested in casting blame. When it is not ignored, the answers can vary, but they are mostly ones that invoke a significant role for government. The interesting aspect of this answer is that critics do not suggest that we somehow convince private producers to act on the basis of something other than profit, but that instead we replace them with presumably other-motivated bureaucrats or use said bureaucrats to limit severely the choices open to producers. The implicit assumption, of course, is that the government actors in question will not be motivated by profits or self-interest in the same way as the private sector producers are.

How realistic this assumption is remains highly questionable. Why should we assume that government actors are any less self-interested than private sector ones, especially when the door between the two sectors is constantly revolving? And, if government actors do act in their self-interest and are motivated by the political analogy of profits (for example, votes, power, budgets), will they produce results that are any better than the private sector? If blaming the profit motive means giving government a bigger role in solving the problem in question, what assurance can critics of the profit motive provide that political actors will be any less self-interested and that their self-interest will produce any better results?

The critics of proposals to give the private sector a larger role in providing education rarely take a deep look at the pathologies of government provision, preferring instead to blame the well-documented failures of state education on not having 'the right people in charge' or not spending enough money to hire good teachers or get the right resources. Never do they ask the difficult questions about whether these failures are due to structural problems with the way incentives guide behaviour in the political process. To blame the profit motive without asking the comparative institutional question of whether an alternative will do better at solving the problems supposedly caused by the profit motive is to bias the case against the private sector.

The absence of prices and profits

Even this argument, however, does not go far enough. We are still, after all, focused on intentions and motivation. What critics of the profit motive almost never ask is the question of how, in the absence of prices, profits and other market institutions, producers will be able to know what to produce and how to produce it. The profit motive is a crucial part of a broader system that enables producers and consumers to share knowledge in ways that other systems do not.

Suppose for the moment that we have an educational system run by political actors who are not self-interested in the slightest. They genuinely wish to do what's best for the education of young people. For many critics of the profit motive, the problem is solved. We have public-spirited political actors in place of the profit-seeking private sector, so we have taken the profit motive out of education. Well, not so fast. How is it, exactly, that the political actors will know how to allocate resources in the industry? How will they know how much of what kind of education people want? And, more importantly, how will they know how to produce that education without wasting resources in the process? Should we require eight years of education of everyone? Twelve years? Sixteen years? What is the optimal student–teacher ratio? Should we teach phonics or whole language? Should we focus on general education or more practical kinds of skills? What is the ideal balance between subjects? What is the optimal length of the school day or school year? And, most importantly, how will political decision-makers know whether they answer these questions correctly or not?

In markets with good institutions, profit-seeking producers are able to get answers to these questions by observing prices and their own profits and losses to determine which uses of resources are more or less valuable. Rather than having one solution imposed upon all producers, based on the best guesses of political actors, an industry populated by profit-motivated producers can try out alternative solutions and learn which ones work most effectively. Competition for profit is a process of learning and discovery. For all the concerns by critics of the profit motive that allocating resources by profits leads to waste, few if any understand the ways in which profits and prices signal the efficiency of resource use and allow producers to learn from those signals. The waste associated with state-provided education, such as the bloated administrative bureaucracy, is a product of this system lacking the signals of profit and loss to indicate when resources are being wasted. The superiority of the profit motive is that it provides producers with this kind of reliable signal about how efficiently they are using resources, at least when the institutional structure is right. The strength of the market and the weakness of government provision is not that business people are smarter than bureaucrats; it is that the very same people will generate better results in the market because the market gives them prices and profits as 'aids to the mind' to guide their resource allocation decisions.

More than just a motive

It is this last point which is the real problem with the focus on the profit motive: it assumes that the primary role of profits is motivating (or in contemporary language 'incentivising') producers. If one takes that view, it might be seen as relatively easy to find other ways to motivate them or to design a new system where production is taken over by the state. If the more important role of profits is to communicate knowledge about the efficiency of resource use and enable producers to learn what they are doing well or poorly, however, the argument becomes much more complicated. Now the critics must explain what, in the absence of profits, will tell producers what they should and should not do. How will producers know not just what to produce but what inputs to use to produce it? Profits and losses perform this communicative function. Eliminating profit-seeking from an industry does not just require that a new incentive be found but that a new way of learning be developed as well. Profit is not just a 'motive', it is integral to the irreplaceable social learning process of the market. The very phrase 'the profit motive' reveals the critics' focus on motivation rather than the systemic communicative role played by profits and losses.

Saying that we shouldn't operate by the profit motive in education or any other industry is a nice-sounding slogan that suggests that the good or service in question should not be produced according to the self-interest of private sector actors. The critics who invoke such arguments often argue that the good or service should be distributed on some basis other than what is 'profitable'. This claim is rarely followed by an explanation of what criteria will be used to allocate the good and how exactly producers of the good will know what goods or services people want and how to produce them in ways that waste the fewest resources possible.

If profit-seeking producers operate in an institutional framework that produces profit signals that reliably coordinate their choices over outputs and inputs with the preferences of consumers, their 'motives' are largely irrelevant. Even the most knave-like will be led, by the famed invisible hand, to do the right thing. By giving profit and loss a larger role in education, we could eliminate the wastes of state provision and begin to discover exactly what sort of education, produced with what sorts of inputs, best serves the needs of parents and students. 'Keeping the profit motive out' sounds like the equivalent of giving the Tin Man from Oz a heart, when in fact it's much more like Oedipus gouging out his own eyes.

PART 2: LESSONS FROM THE UK AND ABROAD

3 SETTING UP A FREE SCHOOL

Toby Young

We ought to ponder the fact that there is nothing more difficult to manage, more dubious to accomplish, or more dangerous to execute than the introduction of new institutions; for the innovator makes enemies of everyone who is well off under the old order, and has unenthusiastic supporters among those who would be well off in the new order.

Niccolo Machiavelli, *The Prince*

In August 2009, I wrote an article for the *Observer* in which I said I wanted to set up a state secondary school that had a similar ethos and curriculum to an old-fashioned grammar but was accessible to all, regardless of income, ability or faith. I called it a 'comprehensive grammar'. Within 48 hours of the article's publication, I had been contacted by over 150 people offering to help. I convened a public meeting at my house and forty people squeezed into my sitting room. Out of that group, a fifteen-person steering committee emerged. I was in business.

We decided our best bet was to try to set up an academy under the then Labour government's scheme to allow taxpayer-funded schools to be established with some independence from local authority control. However, we wanted our school to deviate from the standard academy model in three respects: it would be sponsored by a group of parents and teachers; the ownership and operation of the school would be kept separate, with the school owned by a charitable trust but operated by an experienced education provider, either a charity or a for-profit company; and it would lease a school building, ideally from a commercial property company. I now realise that this was naive. Trying to set up an academy that was new in just one respect was ambitious enough.

Sponsored by a group of parents and teachers

The difficulties we faced here largely arose out of the fact that we were a group of unpaid volunteers with no experience of setting up schools. Setting up a taxpayer-funded primary school is hard. Setting up a taxpayer-funded secondary school is even harder. The majority of the 24 'free schools' that opened in September 2011 under the coalition government's new scheme for the establishment of independent, taxpayer-funded schools were primaries. I am not surprised that only 203 academies were set up under the last government and that the majority of them converted from state schools. None of them was set up by a group of unpaid volunteers.

Only two taxpayer-funded secondary schools were established by groups of parents under the last Labour government: the Elmgreen School in Lambeth and JCoSS (the Jewish Community Secondary School) in Barnet. Both are voluntary-aided comprehensives and are funded via their local authorities rather than directly by the Department for Education. It took the group in South London four years; it took the group in North London ten years. Jonathan Fingerhut, one of the leaders of the Jewish group, told us that aiming to get our school open in just two years was unrealistic, given the amount of labour involved and the pace at which education officials usually work. He suggested that we would be better off aiming for a September 2012 opening – and even that was ambitious.

But Fingerhut's group was at a disadvantage: Labour was in power when it was trying to set up JCoSS. Successive Labour education secretaries paid lip-service to the idea of parents setting up secondary schools – Ed Balls, the Secretary of State for Education from 2007 to 2010, claimed to be in favour of it – but in reality no official procedure was put in place for them to follow. Both Jonathan Fingerhut's group and the group in Lambeth succeeded only thanks to the unstinting support of Andrew Adonis, an education minister from 2005 to 2008, and by the time we arrived on the scene he had moved to a different department.

Under Gordon Brown, the only funding route available to groups that wanted to set up new academies was the Building Schools for the Future (BSF) programme. In order to qualify for BSF funding, the first thing you needed to do was prove that there was a basic need for additional school places in your borough – that there was insufficient capacity in the borough's existing state secondary schools to accommodate the anticipated growth in demand in the future. That turned out to be relatively straightforward, thanks to the population boom caused by Labour's open-door immigration policy.

More difficult was persuading the local authority to endorse our proposal for a new academy. One of the first things Ed Balls did on becoming Secretary of State was to strengthen the oversight local authorities enjoyed over the setting up of new academies. Indeed, academy sponsors could not even enter the set-up process without their local authority's consent. Before you could get to first base, the Education Department had to write a 'Letter of Intent' to the local authority outlining the plans for a new school as outlined by the academy sponsor, and the Department wasn't prepared to do that without the local authority's blessing. Local authorities, of course, aren't keen on any moves that reduce their control over education in the locality – though there are exceptions.

We were in the midst of a long and seemingly interminable negotiation with the London Borough of Ealing when the general election was called in 2010. From my group's point of view, one of the most attractive aspects of the Conservatives' education policy was the proposal to remove the local authority veto over the setting up of new academies. In the five days that followed the election, I tracked the Conservative–Liberal Democrat talks closely, trying to discover the status of the local authority veto. Would the Liberal Democrats insist it remain in place as part of the 'coalition agreement'? It was not until 24 hours after Michael Gove's appointment as Secretary of State for Education that we learned the veto had gone.

After the change of government, setting up a parent-and-teacher-sponsored academy became a bit easier – it was one of the coalition's flagship policies, after all – but it was far from plain sailing. Local authorities can still make things difficult for voluntary groups like mine, even without a formal veto – for instance, by refusing to grant planning consent for a new school. There is also the opposition of the teaching unions to deal with, as well as other ideologically hostile groups.

The biggest obstacle of all, however, is the sheer complexity of the process. The word 'process' is misleading. It implies that there is a procedure that can be followed, with a clear set of rules: something fixed. You enter it with a proposal; you pass through a series of numbered stages; you emerge at the other end with a school.

In fact, it's more like a maze. A maze designed by Escher. You try to work your way through the bureaucratic labyrinth as best you can, but the ground keeps shifting beneath your feet. Since the change of government, officials within the Department have done their best to guide groups like mine through the maze, but the 'process' is so fiendishly complex that they often do not fully grasp it themselves. Part of the problem is that the legal and regulatory framework is continually evolving. You are told you must follow the rules, but no one seems to know what they are. There are various fixed points to navigate by – Acts of Parliament, High Court judgements, EU procurement rules – but the language in which they're written – official, legalistic, precise – is misleading. These documents are both internally inconsistent and mutually inconsistent. No two people agree on what is and is not allowed. Everything is subject to interpretation.

'Welcome to my world,' said my brother-in-law when I complained about this. My brother-in-law is the chief legal counsel of BP. He has a tough job, but setting up a free school is, in some ways, tougher. In the course of trying to establish an oil refinery in the Caucasus, he has only to familiarise himself with the legal and regulatory framework in the region. He can leave the finances to the CFO and the politics to his boss. And they each have several hundred employees at their beck and call and vast resources at their disposal. I was just one person with an iPhone and a laptop.

In the course of trying to establish a free school, I had to familiarise myself with every aspect of the process: the ministers and their special advisers; the Free Schools Directorate; the Outline Business Case; the Funding Agreement; and so on. Then there is the army of educational consultancies and agencies you have to deal with, all professing to have expertise within one of several dozen fields: literacy, inclusion, SEN, SEAL, EAL, EBD (it does not take long to run into an acronym storm). As for the property side, there are the architects, the planners, the chartered surveyors, the quantity surveyors, the contractors. Not to mention the Building Bulletins. Don't get me started on the Building Bulletins ...

I was able to delegate some of this work to the people on my steering committee, but they were all volunteers, too. You cannot tell someone who is not being paid to have Ealing Council's Pupil Place Planning projections for 2010–2020 on your desk first thing tomorrow morning. You have to do it yourself, even if it involves staying up all night. Big society = little sleep.

In *The Last Tycoon*, F. Scott Fitzgerald says of his hero, the studio chief Monroe Stahr, that he is one of the few people in Hollywood capable of keeping 'the whole equation' in his head. I was unable to keep the whole equation in my head. The words of Sandy Nuttgens, the leader of the parent group that set up the Elmgreen School in Lambeth, kept coming back to haunt me: 'For four years, I felt like I was on a vertical learning curve.'

Outsourcing the day-to-day operation of the school

This brings me to the second respect in which the West London Free School would differ from the standard academy model: we wanted to subcontract the day-to-day management of the school to an established education provider. I thought that once we had an experienced provider on board, it would do the lion's share of the work. I could take on a more strategic role, surveying the field of battle from my vantage point on a hilltop rather than grubbing about in the mud.

We ran a procurement process, producing a very professional-looking 'Request for Proposal' (RFP) and an *Official Journal of the European Union* (OJEU) notice. All the usual organisations interested in this line of work submitted proposals: the Centre for British Teachers (CfBT), Cognita, EdisonLearning, GEMS Education, International English Schools (IES), Kunskapsskolan, Nord Anglia, Serco and the Vosper Thornycroft (VT) group. We even had some applications from less obvious places: Collingwood, Creative Learning and Haberdashers' Aske's. We then put together an evaluation matrix and prepared to score the different bids with a view to selecting a winner. Before shortlisting, however, I thought it would be prudent to ask a solicitor to look over our procurement process. Was it watertight?

He thought that what we had done so far was fairly robust but advised us that if we went ahead and appointed a service provider we would run the risk of being challenged. He was not too worried about a case being brought by a disappointed bidder – though that was a possibility – but he was concerned by a challenge from a politically motivated individual who opposed the free schools policy. Such a challenge would probably fail, but that would not deter such a person from mounting a challenge, particularly if he or she was eligible for legal aid.

The risk was particularly high for our group since it was the one with the highest public profile. If the political opponents of the policy could find a legal mechanism for making our lives more difficult and delaying the establishment of our school, it was clear that they would not hesitate to use it. Our conclusion was that we did not want to be the canary in the mine shaft.

Leasing a site

Deciding not to enter into a partnership with an experienced education provider made leasing a building considerably more difficult. This was the third respect in which the West London Free School would deviate from the standard Academy model: we wanted to lease a building.

Our problem was that the charitable trust that would own the school had no credit history: it has zero covenant strength. And while the Department said it was prepared to guarantee a per capita amount to cover the cost of leasing a building, it was reluctant to guarantee the annual rent if we ended up undersubscribed, i.e. with fewer pupils than there were places. We did not think we would be, obviously, but we could not guarantee that we would not be: at least not to the satisfaction of a commercial property company.

We had hoped to solve this problem by getting our service provider to stand behind the lease, but that was no longer an option. Even if a commercial property company was prepared to take a risk and lease a building to us, it would build that risk into the annual rent. That would make the rent unaffordable. Then I had a brainwave: why not lease a public building? No, I am not talking about a building owned by a local authority in London: I am talking about one owned by the Royal Kingdom of Saudi Arabia.

We found an empty secondary school on the Ealing/Hounslow border that was owned by the Saudi government. We approached the embassy and, after receiving advice from a Saudi official on how to structure our proposal, submitted an offer to HRH Prince Mohammed bin Nawaf, the ambassador to the United Kingdom and Republic of Ireland. This was in the spring of 2010.

We still have not had a reply. We made some discreet enquiries and discovered the reason no one has responded is because the Kingdom has never had a request to lease a government-owned building before. The Ministry of Foreign Affairs in Riyadh simply had no idea how to process it. No process, no response.

In the absence of being able to guarantee a lease agreement, our best bet was to find a building that the Department for Education would be prepared to purchase on our behalf. This was a less attractive option than leasing because it would give the Department the whip-hand in any future negotiations over the independence of our school. We knew that, if the Department bought our site for us, our Funding Agreement with the Secretary of State would contain a reversion clause whereby ownership of the site would revert to the Department in the event of our funding being cut off. In effect, the Department would be our landlord, regardless of whose name appeared on the deeds.

Still, it looked as if we did not have any choice so we started searching for a suitably inexpensive site. My hopes were raised when I was summoned to a meeting with the lead member for Children's Services at the London Borough of Hammersmith and Fulham, who told me she knew of a potential site. Unfortunately, it turned out to be for a primary, not a secondary, school. But at that meeting I was introduced to John McIntosh, the ex-head of the London Oratory School, who was now working as an education consultant for the council. I invited him to lunch and he agreed to join our steering committee. Not long afterwards, he told me that the council had announced its intention to sell a building in Hammersmith called Palingswick House – a former school. He thought that it might be suitable for a small secondary school.

After a protracted negotiation, the Department agreed a price with Hammersmith and Fulham Council and, on 1 March 2011, we became the first free school to sign a Funding Agreement with the Secretary of State. The West London Free School saw the first pupils passing through its gates in September 2011, and I'm happy to report that, far from being undersubscribed, we're oversubscribed by 9:1.

The reason my group pulled it off, I think, is because we realised that, after a good deal of trial and error, our best hope was if we departed as little as possible from the 'process' that the Department had put in place to set up academies under the previous government.

Trying to create a centrally funded secondary school that was sponsored by a group of parents and teachers as opposed to an established academies operator was ambitious enough. Trying to reinvent the wheel at the same time by outsourcing the management of the school to a third party and leasing the building was simply unrealistic. If you are going to do something new, do not try to do too many new things at once.

Conclusion

Thanks to the complexity of the process, the scarcity of suitable sites and the government's limited capital expenditure budget, I cannot see more than a few hundred free schools being established in the lifetime of this parliament. The number of parent-and-teacher-sponsored free schools is likely to be a fraction of this, with the majority being set up by existing multi-academy sponsors like ARK and Harris. That is particularly true given that the Department has now tightened up the approval process and requires free school proposers to do a huge amount of preparatory work before they are eligible for any paid support from the Department. Under the new rules, my group would have persevered and eventually prevailed, but it would have taken us longer.

The obvious solution is to enable for-profit companies to set up, own and operate free schools provided they soak up all the capital costs. Given the opposition of the Liberal Democrats, the only way that is likely to happen is if the Conservatives win an outright majority at the next general election – and even then, I regret to say, it's far from certain.

Allowing profit-making free schools would have many advantages, quite apart from all the usual economic advantages of facilitating the profit motive in any sector of life. If profit-making firms could own schools, they could invest the capital and take the equity risk of failure: if the school were successful, the sponsor would make more profit; if it were not, it would make a loss. Currently, there is no body able to take any equity risk, so obtaining a site is extremely difficult. Allowing profit-making providers would also create economies of scale in overcoming the regulatory and bureaucratic obstacles to free schools so that each applicant did not have to reinvent the wheel or rely on the advice of government officials. Allowing profit-making bodies would also reduce the regulatory burden because groups of parents would not have to go through the artificial process of setting up a trust to own a school while co-opting a profit-making body to run a school.

There is a halfway house that could be adopted as an interim measure. The reason we were not able to subcontract the operation of our school to a service provider is because the risk of legal challenge was too great. The Department could mitigate that risk by setting up a procurement framework, or something similar, that would allow free school proposers to enter into partnerships with experienced partners. The companies in the framework need not all be for-profits education management organisations, either. I suspect the large charitable providers, including some of the academy operators, would want to be included. The involvement of some commercial providers, however, would not be a deal-breaker for the Liberal Democrats provided the schools they ended up operating were owned by charitable trusts.

Once a proposer group had formed a partnership with an experienced provider, establishing a free school would be comparatively easy. It would no longer be dependent on the labour of unpaid volunteers with no experience of setting up schools. It would also save the taxpayer money. My group has been able to get over the final hurdle only by working with a Project Management Company appointed – and financed – by the government. That is a cost that could be borne by the provider.

It would also make leasing a building from a commercial property company easier, since the provider could stand behind the lease. Leasing commercial buildings might not be the most cost-effective way of setting up free schools from the taxpayers' point of view – in the long run, it is probably cheaper to buy existing school buildings from local authorities – but it would certainly mean many more free schools could be established in any given year. The number would not be limited by the Department's annual capital expenditure budget.

Will the Department put a procurement framework in place that will enable free schools to enter into relationships with experienced providers? The direction of travel within Whitehall is to shy away from the public–private partnerships that the previous government was so keen on. But if Michael Gove is serious about wanting free schools sponsored by parents and teachers to become a significant part of the overall pattern of taxpayer-funded education, he is going to have to work out a way to enable the large providers to play a bigger role. I hope he does, because if this government turns out to be a one-term government, a few hundred free schools are unlikely to have a significant impact on public education, but several thousand could create a sustainable revolution.

I am grateful that the free school model enabled my school to open in September, but disappointed that the procedure for establishing parent-and-teacher-sponsored free schools has been made harder rather than easier since the coalition was elected. It is symptomatic of an ever-increasing aversion to risk that is characteristic of the government, particularly when it comes to reforming public services. Often, the way Conservative ministers explain this timidity is to point to their Liberal Democrat colleagues and claim that a more aggressive programme of public service reform would not be politically possible. But perhaps both they and their Liberal colleagues are overestimating the political risks. I will close by quoting a passage from *A Journey*, Tony Blair's memoirs, in which the former prime minister describes the typical passage of a reform: 'The change is proposed; it is denounced as a disaster; it proceeds with vast chipping away and opposition; it is unpopular; it comes about; within a short space of time it is as if it has always been so.'

4 THE PROFIT MOTIVE IN SWEDISH EDUCATION

Peje Emilsson

I first unveiled a plan to launch for-profit independent schools to the board of the Swedish Free Enterprise Foundation in October 1999 – eight years after the introduction of the pioneering school voucher system in Sweden. As a member of the board, I argued that the time was right to start a chain of for-profit schools and gave it the compelling name of 'Kunskapsskolan' (which means 'the Knowledge School' in Swedish). One of my colleagues on the board, a well-known Swedish economist, who later became a member of parliament, reacted at once. 'But Peje,' she said, 'you can't run schools for profit – education is beyond that.' Even the suggestion that you should be able to make a profit from running a state-funded school, just as you can make a profit from being a private contractor assigned to build a state school, was considered somewhat outlandish.

But why is it that the profit motive has such a pejorative connotation when combined with education, when the facts tell a very different story? The work of Professor James Tooley shows how private and for-profit schools attain far better results in educating poor children in Third World countries than available state school alternatives. A 2009 Harvard University study (by Paul E. Peterson and Matthew M. Chingos) on scholastic achievement at for-profit and not-for-profit charter schools in the USA shows that schools do much better under for-profit than under non-profit management. Sweden's experience certainly adds compelling evidence to these findings and I believe that the 'received wisdom' that the profit motive and education do not mix is now increasingly being exposed as unfounded.

The one-size-fits-all monolithic system

In Sweden in the 1970s, government schools had become instruments for a social policy for achieving equality rather than education. The policy of offering a 'one-size-fits-all' school created a monolithic system, wherein all students were viewed as having the same needs and were to be taught in the same way. With the exception of a few private schools, open only to those children whose parents could afford the high tuition costs, almost all schools were operated by the public sector. Although the promise of the high-tax welfare state was to ensure a good education for all, in practice it achieved the opposite result. Students who came from families with no academic tradition – i.e. working-class or lower-middle-class children – came off worst. Sweden was going downhill on all international measures of education results.

A wider political debate in the late 1980s on the need for education reforms, including the freedom to choose, was fuelled by the example of parents struggling to preserve small village schools in rural areas. The message that emerged was clear: let the parents keep the fixed, tax-funded amount in the local municipal budget that was set aside for their children's education, neither more nor less, and let them organise a more cost-efficient, effective school operation. Hence the idea of the voucher was becoming established.

One important part of the centre-right government's agenda

for change in 1991 was the introduction of a school voucher system. The simple thought behind the reform was to promote higher-quality instruction and better overall results by enabling a higher degree of educational pluralism and competition. Following the experiences of educational reforms of the 1970s, the government also wanted a vehicle for innovation and the development of methodology in schools, without experimenting with the whole generation in state schools at a particular time. It gave parents and students the right to choose the school that would enable the student to realise his or her potential, regardless of the family's economic status. Despite the Social Democrats initially being opposed to the new reforms, they later not only accepted the voucher system when they returned to power in 1994, they also increased the compensation level from 85 per cent of the average cost of a pupil in a local state school to 100 per cent. Today there is widespread public and political acceptance of the voucher programme and the emerging for-profit school market.

The Swedish voucher system

The Swedish school voucher system consists of five basic parts:

- There is a core curriculum which all schools receiving government funds must follow. The National Schools Inspectorate monitors compliance and assesses quality.
- Authorised independent schools are state-funded by a per pupil allowance – a voucher for each student who chooses that particular school. The National Schools Inspectorate alone makes the decisions on authorisation. Local authorities

can object – and they frequently do – but they cannot veto the decision.

- The voucher amount is paid by each local authority and varies between municipalities depending on differences in costs. National legislation prescribes that the local authorities are obliged to pay the independent school an amount which corresponds to the average cost for a pupil in the local state school which the pupil would otherwise have attended. This means that independent schools do not increase government spending per pupil on education – they just redistribute it, according to parents' and students' choices. We call it a 'voucher', but technically the independent schools invoice the local authorities directly, based on information about the number of students they enrol.
- Independent schools are not allowed to charge additional fees. As a result, they cannot pick and choose students, but have to accept them on a 'first-come-first-served' basis.
- Within the framework of the curriculum, independent schools are free to organise their own programmes, timetables and pedagogical methods. The free school reform was accompanied by deregulation, going from a system whereby the government regulated inputs down to the size of a classroom to a system whereby the government monitors results and outcomes but gives a higher degree of freedom for methods and inputs.

Independent schools have gone from being a rare exception to an important part of the Swedish educational system. Before the reform in 1991, fewer than 1 per cent of children aged seven to sixteen were enrolled in private schools. Today, that figure has increased to 11 per cent. In upper secondary education – ages sixteen to eighteen – the trend has been even more pronounced: from around 1 per cent of all students in 1991 up to 23 per cent in 2011. In certain regions of the country (primarily in the Greater Stockholm area) almost half of all students are enrolled in independent schools. Overall, one out of five Swedish schools is an independent school, and almost half of them differ from state schools in their pedagogical approach. More than 60 per cent of independent schools are run as for-profit limited companies.

The most important aspect of the voucher reform and the new education market is that students at independent schools do better academically than in the state schools. One measure of results is called 'merit value'. This is the average value of marks pupils receive. The maximum value possible at the compulsory school level is 320 points, reflecting the highest marks in all subjects. In the spring of 2011, the average merit value of ninth-grade leavers in all Swedish compulsory schools – state and independent – was 211 points. In independent schools alone it was 229.

Another measure is the national tests in key subjects that are conducted in all schools and corrected according to a national standard. Here as well, independent school students clearly do better. This pattern repeats itself in upper secondary education. And, remember: independent schools are not, at any level of the educational system, allowed to choose their students. According to a multitude of surveys, parents, teachers and students say they are more satisfied with independent schools. The teachers' unions in Sweden understandably today also accept the school choice reform, as it now provides their members with more employment opportunities.

At the same time, state schools are being helped by the

competition. Different studies of education results in localities where independent schools have been established have shown that state schools in these cities are more efficient and successful than the national average. This is simply because they needed to improve in order to compete with the independent schools. Otherwise they would lose students and the per-student grants from the state school budget.

Of course, not every independent school is good. Even if the freedom to choose means that parents and children can easily leave schools that underperform, the government has to constantly improve inspection and control mechanisms (for both independent and state schools). As with any market carved out of an old monopoly, there is a need to follow developments closely. Summing up the overall results of Sweden's eighteen years of experience with the school voucher and a competitive education market, there can be no doubt that the independent schools have given taxpayers greater value for the money spent on education. This is true both in their own capacity – on average, they have better quality and results – and as catalysts of improvement in the state schools they challenge. Competition works.

Kunskapsskolan – a modern alternative

Kunskapsskolan started its first five schools in 2000, and by 2011 the chain had grown to 33 upper-secondary schools. With approximately 10,000 students and 800 employees we are one of Sweden's five largest school chain companies. When we started Kunskapsskolan, our ambition was to create a modern alternative to the conventional 'one-size-fits-all' factory school. Today's schools prepare children for a dramatically different labour market and life than that for which the conventional school was designed at the end of the nineteenth century. Better organisation, modern technology and continual development of processes now provide new opportunities to personalise education. That was our idea, and it was based on the belief that every child can grow far beyond what we think is possible, if recognised as a unique individual.

When a twelve-year-old child enrols at one of our schools, we invest time and resources to help tailor the curriculum and learning environment to meet his or her particular needs and ambitions. Each student has a dedicated coach and together with their teachers and parents they set short- and long-term goals. Strategies are then developed for reaching the goals, performance is assessed and strategies adjusted accordingly.

The result is a system wherein no child is left behind and no child's learning progression is held back. The ability to work towards goals, design strategies and measure performance is something that comes with it. This is the very foundation of lifelong learning and the modern working life. In close cooperation with the teachers' unions, we have aligned the organisation of the teachers' work with our pedagogical programme. As a result, Kunskapsskolan's teachers can spend 50 per cent more time on educating and coaching students than in conventional schools. Our teachers spend less time preparing lessons thanks to the extensive support system, giving them the ability to spend more time with the pupils. This method of working is common among all our school units, giving us a great tool for continual development and improvement. Regularly and systematically we share our experience between units to identify best practices. In every respect, students benefit from the best possible learning achievement of the whole corporation, not only of their own school.

In one way, however, every single school we run can be seen as a separate, albeit small, company. The principal's sole task is to deliver high-quality education according to the goals of the school and the company as a whole. The only restriction is that we cannot use more than 95 per cent of the voucher revenue. In order to relieve principals of all distractions, Kunskapsskolan has one corporate back office which handles all support operations, such as marketing, administration, financial and human resources.

How is Kunskapsskolan faring? For our compulsory school pupils completing the ninth and last grade, the average 'merit value' was 237 points in the spring of 2011 (out of a maximum of 320 points), compared with the national average of 211 and the independent school average of 229 in the spring of 2011. Fifteen of our 21 compulsory schools which graduated ninth-grade classes in the spring of 2010 were graded the best schools in their respective city, municipality or neighbourhood. Nineteen of the 21 were placed among the top three.

There are a number of factors behind the success of the Swedish model in general and Kunskapsskolan in particular. First, the Swedish free school and voucher model has provided families with alternatives and provided schools with incentives for improvement. It has saved Swedish society from a situation of having a completely segregated school system, with a monolithic state system providing few choices and a completely separate private system for those who can afford it. But just as important as the diversity and alternatives this system creates is the fact that the Swedish model is – unlike most other systems for creating educational diversity – market-driven. The question of whether a new school will succeed or fail now depends on the choice of customers – students and families – not of politicians or civil servants.

The second factor is that the Swedish system focuses on results and performance and not on whether the legal entity is for-profit or non-profit. The reimbursements to independent schools are, as mentioned above, based on the average cost for a student in the local state schools calculated on the basis of current student enrolment. If an independent school exhibits a higher degree of occupancy of its 'seats' than the average state school enrolment, it creates a surplus, a profit. And only a higher degree of perceived quality can create this higher degree of enrolment. Independent schools will become sustainable and profitable only if they provide a better quality of service than the existing state schools.

A more rational organisation of resources, a more efficient administration, the teacher–student ratio and other input factors can affect costs, but they can never in the long run provide a profitable school if they do not contribute to an attractive offering and high perceived quality. I am convinced that without this possibility of making a profit – and compensating owners and investors for risks through dividends to shareholders – we would not have independent schools outperforming the old state school monopoly and setting new long-term standards for improved education.

Without the right for it to be a for-profit company, Kunskapsskolan's model would not have been developed. The private owners have invested approximately 125 million SEK (around £11 million) in developing the company, and it was not until 2010, year nine of the company's operations, that accumulated profits surpassed accumulated losses. Would these heavy financial burdens have been taken on without a theoretical future possibility of refund?

Starting a school requires both capital and talent. Premises need to be obtained and staff hired before a single student enrols. We do not own the buildings where our schools operate, but they must conform to our specifications for the architecture and the interior. For example, we do not have traditional classrooms; larger and smaller work rooms have glass walls and there are a lot of open spaces with individual work stations. This means we have to find property where the owners are willing to invest heavily in order to renovate according to our detailed demands. In return, we need to start out by signing fifteen-year lease agreements – without knowing whether we will have enough pupils to even meet our fixed costs. This is a large economic risk for the school and its owners. It is a risk we are prepared to take, however, because we believe in the unique contribution we are making to education.

But if that is the case, why then should we not be allowed to make a profit through providing pupils with high-quality education? And why, if our clients are satisfied and we meet, or exceed, scholastic requirements, should a possible surplus not be distributed at the owners' discretion to give a return on the original investments and risks? 'Because the funding is from taxpayers' money' is the answer from those who naively believe we can have innovation through entrepreneurship in education without entrepreneurs.

But taxpayers' money is already widely used throughout the state sector to compensate product and service providers that make profits. Defence industry products, buses and trains for public transportation, medicines in healthcare and coffee for local treasury staff, to pick just a few examples, are all produced by profitable private companies and are paid for by government funding in a system that is accepted as quite natural. And, again, what is the difference between using taxpayers' money to finance privately owned, profitable companies that put up the school buildings or produce the textbooks on the one hand and, on the other hand, using taxpayers' money out of the same government budget to pay those who organise and offer education itself?

The new Swedish model

As well as being an entrepreneur, I am also a parent, a citizen and a taxpayer. As a parent I want to be able to decide what kind of education best meets the requirements of my own children, as I know them better than anyone else. In doing so, I want choices. As a citizen I want all children, regardless of background, to have the best education possible, which is suited to their needs. I want the education system to function in such a way that innovation and constant improvement are natural conditions. And as a taxpayer, I want value for the money that I pay to finance government services. In education, value for money is indicated by the knowledge and skills students acquire to build a good life for themselves and make a contribution to society. If certain schools can make a profit from outperforming those that do not, I want my tax money to be used exactly in those win-win operations that benefit both the student and society. My firm belief is that not only is the Kunskapsskolan system suitable for export, the whole Swedish school voucher system is as well.

In the middle of the twentieth century, the term 'Swedish model' came to relate to a unique public–private partnership in labour market relations that ensured stable economic growth, private prosperity and shared social benefits. Today, I would say, we are developing the 'New Swedish Model'. It is also a public–private partnership, but relates to the way the collective social benefits are distributed. Government funding through taxes secures equal rights for all to receive services such as healthcare and education. At the same time, a readiness to permit private and public actors to compete in providing those services gives people free choice and secures a far-reaching individualisation of the way these services are provided. In Sweden this 'client choice' or 'voucher' model is now being extended into healthcare, child-care/kindergarten and elderly care services, with a widespread political consensus.

In education, there is a need, and room, for many different actors, including for-profit education companies. The goal is to create sound preconditions for innovation and more successful educational concepts. In achieving this we need to welcome all contributors. The 'New Swedish Model', with its openness to profitable independent schools, can lead the way.

5 THE STORY OF A SCHOOL ENTREPRENEUR

Barbara Bergstrom

When Sweden's non-socialist government introduced the 'free school reform' in 1992, the word 'free' had four connotations. As an educator, you were *free to start* your own school, after meeting certain basic requirements set out by the National Schools Inspectorate. Secondly, as a parent and student, you were *free to choose* a school with the profile you preferred and not forced to attend a government school by local officials. Thirdly, the school of choice was completely *free of fees*, and so there was no additional cost when choosing a school offered by a cooperative, a trust or a company. Finally, free schools have more *freedom in pedagogic ideas and in the daily running of the school*, including autonomy from municipal school boards. All of these freedoms interact, and so the freedom to choose becomes a reality only when there is the freedom to offer alternatives. Equal freedom to choose is also a reality only when education as such is free. And a degree of autonomy in running a school is necessary if you are to be successful in creating a school in accordance with your own strong convictions.

Setting up a new school

I definitely had such convictions, so after parliament had decided to introduce the reform, I resigned as a teacher in a government school in order to start my own school. I found a suitable building in Stockholm and then applied and subsequently received a permit. After inviting a former colleague to join the project I set up a company, which we considered to be the most effective form for managing and leading such an organisation. When starting the first school in August 1993, I had three major convictions:

- English is the world's common language and Swedish children should learn to command English at an early age. This is best done through language immersion, performed by native English-speaking teachers, and extending to subjects such as maths and science.
- Discipline and a calm and safe environment in school are necessary prerequisites for learning. Strong principals must create an orderly environment in which teachers can teach and students learn. 'Tough love' became the motto for a school which is strict in norms for behaviour, but out of love for the students and with a strong determination to help each child succeed.
- There should be high academic expectations of students. The assumption must be that every child can achieve, irrespective of social background. Also the most talented students should be challenged to reach their full potential. Regular assessment forms the basis for correcting problems early. Mentor teachers, in charge of fifteen students each, call parents every second week to report and also to receive feedback.

To achieve these goals, it was necessary to show strong and clear leadership, to recruit the best teachers and to make it possible for those teachers to focus on teaching by securing an orderly environment with minimum distraction. There is a strict dress code and mobile phones, music players and chewing gum are not allowed. These rules are soon internalised and become a natural part of an orderly environment focused on learning.

The alternative we presented at 'Engelska Skolan' (English School), as it was called at the time, proved to be popular among parents, and the school was full in a relatively short period of time. A major reason was that our concept stood in direct contrast to the 'feel-good curriculum' and the 'anything goes', 'no adult authority' attitudes which were dominant in the state schools at the time. Following the anti-authoritarian wave of 1968, Rousseau's views about the good child who could only be hurt by adult intervention came to dominate teacher training colleges, state schools and school authorities in Sweden. Most parents strongly disliked this development.

Even though we filled the school from the start, our finances were still not secure. With no private investment of our own we had to reduce costs where possible. For example, to avoid additional cleaning costs, I went to the school at weekends to do the cleaning myself. And before the school opened, I approached banks, post offices and other companies in Stockholm to ask whether they had any used furniture which they could donate to our school. We were able to equip not only our offices and staff room but also classrooms with used furniture of good quality. I also paid myself very little salary during the first years, until we were on a more solid financial footing.

I am relating this not in order to portray myself as 'Wonderwoman', but as something that comes naturally for many entrepreneurs. You focus on the essentials and minimise costs until you are certain, after several years, that you have secured the basis for success. And success, as I saw it, was to show that my ideas and effort would lead to a really great school. It was certainly not to make a lot of money. My dream was to create my very own school, in the shape and form in which I strongly believed. This would not have been possible if I had stayed in the state school system. Only by setting up my own school, with the freedom to act, could I have achieved what I did.

In 1998, the school was moved to a building in an immigrant area south of Stockholm, where I also started an upper-secondary school. Then, in 2002, I was contacted by the municipality of Järfälla, north of Stockholm, which wanted me to take over and transform a failed government school, also in an immigrant area, which I subsequently did. In 2003, ten years after opening our first school, we decided to expand the business, despite the financial risks involved. We set out to establish three new schools in cities approximately two hours' drive from Stockholm, based only on the limited capital from the mother school. Fortunately, the basic concept (English and order) proved to be attractive, and we soon filled the new schools with students. By 2011, Internationella Engelska Skolan (IES) was educating more than 11,000 students in 17 schools across Sweden – making it the largest free school organisation at the compulsory school level. We are also starting summer schools in the USA and UK and have been selected to manage our first free school in the UK. By 2012/13 we expect to reach a turnover of one billion Swedish krona (approximately £100 million).

The reason I have told my personal story as a school entrepreneur is that it illustrates several basic aspects of allowing private enterprise within the framework of a voucher model for schools. One aspect is that many entrepreneurs, with an educational background, do not start out with the idea of becoming rich. Instead, the driving force is something entirely different: freedom to create your own project and to transform your convictions into reality.

Closely connected with this is my belief that a transformational change is close to impossible within the existing school system. Therefore, if governments wish new ideas to be tested, they have to allow these concepts to be established outside the existing state system. And those offering new ideas have to be able to reach out to parents as their true 'customers', and not be forced to depend upon local school boards, which will almost always throw a wrench into the machinery. It is a complete misunderstanding of the market economy to describe it only as 'profit-driven'. It is often forgotten that a crucial aspect of a 'market' is that it encourages experiments and makes it possible for people with ideas to put them into practice. The outcome will depend on the validity of the ideas and the competence of the people behind them. Without the freedom of the market, however, many excellent ideas and dreams will not reach the testing stage and companies like IES would not exist.

The right to make a profit

A third aspect is that expansion would not happen without the right to make a profit. The reason for this is twofold: *capability* and *incentive.* Only if you have been able to accumulate profits from your first projects are you able to acquire the financial strength to expand. Expansion is costly, and before you receive any revenues from a new school you must invest a considerable amount. You must hire a principal and a school secretary half a year in advance, to undertake the planning for the new school. There are marketing costs and you must buy furniture, equipment, computer systems and books. You have to be able to set up contracts for renovations and buildings, and so on. When we started our real expansion in 2003, not one single contract was accepted by vendors and landlords without the signature and financial stability of the mother company, established through ten years of hard work and accumulated financial solidity. Had we not been allowed to produce and preserve a profit during the first ten years, no expansion could have taken place.

Incentives are also necessary. It is often much easier to maintain the status quo and not expand, as expansion brings new problems and added responsibilities. This is why many excellent schools managed by foundations and cooperatives in Sweden have not expanded. Companies take considerable risks, and the many problems associated with expansion are only worthwhile if these risks and problems are balanced by the possibility of creating value for the future, including financial value.

At this point in the life story of IES, ten years after its creation, I took into account possible value creation, something I had not done initially. I am inclined to believe that this part of the story, too, is quite typical for many entrepreneurs; after many years of hard work to fulfil a dream, but with few material rewards, when there is an opportunity for a major expansion you consider whether or not value would be created by the expansion. In a corporation you act to enhance, and not to destroy, what has been built up already. Without the prospect of value creation, you are much more likely to stay with what you have already established.

Another aspect, probably of major significance too, is that for people with drive, it becomes a proof of success that you are able to create a major company. What you as an owner might do later in life with a capital gain after having sold the company is another story. Entrepreneurs do not necessarily wish to retire in personal luxury. One of my aspirations is to help the Swedish-Tibetan Society provide schools and scholarships in Tibet – an even more challenging environment, and something in which I have long been engaged.

Parents as prime movers

A fourth aspect of the benefit of free schools has to do with the importance of having parents as the true drivers of success of a school and a school company. Only with parental choice at the core of the system can you bypass some of the ingrained political correctness, leftist cultures and bureaucratic obstacles which otherwise will inevitably stop you from doing something really innovative – or just applying plain common sense in education. Political ideas and elite cultures tend to cast a very long shadow. Long after modern neurological research, as well as research on school systems, showed the school 'reformers' in the wake of 1968 to be dangerously wrong, these same 'reformers' still keep a tight grip on the institutions they have conquered – in Sweden, for example, they maintain a tight hold on the national school agencies and on most of the teacher training colleges. Only by placing the full power of choice in the hands of parents, and providing the right to offer alternatives to parents, can you eliminate some of the destructive effects of the established school cultures. Only a full voucher system – based on parental choice and the voucher reimbursement following the student – will achieve this.

Quality creates profits

The fifth and final benefit from free schools that I wish to emphasise has to do with educational quality within the framework of parental choice, a voucher system and for-profit school companies. In public debate, we constantly hear that profits deprive schools of resources for quality education and that a financial surplus can be achieved only by cutting expenditures essential for student success. This is a clear misunderstanding which suggests that those who make such claims have little knowledge about how schools operate in practice.

As noted above, the ability to generate a profit forms a necessary precondition for being able to expand. But how is a profit generated in a school market based on parental choice and voucher payments? It is not by cutting educational resources to the bare bone or by sacrificing quality in education. There is only one way to generate a profit – and that is providing quality education. The financial logic is the following: with a voucher system, financial results depend upon the ability to fill classes to capacity. As each student comes with a voucher payment of roughly 75,000 SEK (approximately £7,500), it makes an enormous difference whether you have 27 students in a class or 30. That difference is, in fact, the entire profit margin. Therefore, in order to fill classes, you must be attractive so that many parents wish to place their children in the school: with vouchers, there is no price restriction for parents – the quality of the school is the only factor to evaluate, beyond travel distance. You also need to build up a waiting list of students, so that you can fill any gaps if a student decides to leave.

How do you establish such a demand for the school? There is only one possible way: by acquiring an excellent reputation, so that many students and parents apply to the school. Education is important for most parents, so they do not take the choice of school lightly. Instead they talk to other parents and discuss what they have seen and heard and scrutinise whether a new school has a good track record. IES has been able to expand because our basic concept is clear, strong and attractive. Parents also see us as being a serious school, based on the people they meet from IES and on our results. The results are far above the national average for schools in Sweden, as well as being far better than for free schools in general, despite our schools having a higher-than-average share of immigrant students.

Following the ability to fill classes (but not beyond the limit where increased numbers affect quality in education), the most important factors for sound financial results are good order in school and classroom management. Quality creates profits and not vice versa.

There is another and perhaps even more vital aspect to the statement that everything starts with quality. Good schools are about finding good people. Therefore, to create a really good school, you have to recruit the best possible principal, who can then recruit and develop excellent teachers. To recruit superb people to work for you, you have to be able to convince them that you are worth working for, and they have to believe in what you stand for. Otherwise they will not come, or stay. It is not profits which are the motivating factor, enticing the best educators to come and work for your organisation. The motivating factors are clarity of purpose and concept, trust in the seriousness of the founder and owner, a strong sense of being part of a stimulating professional community, and the possibility of achieving results above and beyond average. Trust is key – trust in the dedication, competence and basic ideas of the organisation. That trust has to be earned, every week of the year.

During a speech at a conference in Sweden, the legendary C. Northcote Parkinson introduced his 'Swedish Law' on the relationship between growth and employment. It states the following: 'Policies designed to increase production increase employment; policies designed to increase employment do everything but.' My 'Swedish Law' for the education market would state the following: 'School companies successfully aiming for quality in education will also achieve profits; companies primarily aiming for profits at the expense of quality will achieve neither.'

6 THE FORTUNE AT THE BOTTOM OF THE EDUCATION PYRAMID

James B. Stanfield

Since the publication of *The Global Education Industry* (Tooley, 1999), a number of important developments have taken place in this emerging sector which help shed further light on the changing role of the profit motive in the design and delivery of education in low-income communities across the developing world. This chapter will briefly examine the work of the late C. K. Prahalad and its relevance to education; the growth of chains of budget private schools; the development of ecosystems for wealth creation in education; and finally the United Nations and its changing attitude towards the profit motive in education. Lessons for the UK will then be discussed.

C. K. Prahalad and the bottom of the pyramid

The growth and development of budget private schools in developing countries previously documented by James Tooley (Tooley, 2009) has coincided with a more widespread increase in interest in the role of for-profit companies in helping to serve the basic needs of the poor across the developing world. A leading light in documenting this trend over the previous decade was the late C. K. Prahalad (1941–2010), whose publication *The Fortune at the Bottom of the Pyramid: Eradicating Poverty through Profits* (Prahalad, 2004) helped to challenge the complacency of both company directors who were ignoring the majority of the world's population living on low incomes and development experts who have traditionally been highly sceptical about and suspicious of for-profit companies, especially when they attempt to engage with poor communities.[1]

Prahalad rejected the traditional approach to international aid, which often assumed that the poor were helpless victims in desperate need of humanitarian assistance. A new approach was therefore required which recognised that the estimated four billion people who lived at the bottom of the pyramid (BOP) on less than $2 a day were not simply beneficiaries of charitable handouts but resilient entrepreneurs and value-conscious consumers. The strength of this new approach was that it tended to create opportunities for the poor by giving them better access to the products and services that were previously reserved for those on higher incomes. For-profit companies can therefore help to raise the living standards of those at the bottom of the pyramid, while also generating a profit – a genuine win-win situation.

Prahalad highlights the importance of creating the capacity to consume in order to transform low-income communities into consumer markets. Firstly, he is critical of the traditional approach of providing products and services free of charge as this often has the feel of philanthropy: while charity may feel good it

1 Numerous books have been published since, including: Craig Wilson and Peter Wilson, *Make Poverty Business: Increase Profits and Reduce Risks by Engaging with the Poor*, November 2006; Prabhu Kandachar and Minna Halme (eds), *Sustainability Challenges and Solutions at the Base of the Pyramid: Business, Technology and the Poor*, September 2008; Marco Bucheli, *Inclusive Business: A New Strategic Paradigm at the Bottom of the Pyramid Markets: A case study analysis*, 2009; Ted London and Stuart Hart, *Next Generation Business Strategies for the Base of the Pyramid*, November 2010. See the references for full details.

rarely solves the problem in a scalable and sustainable fashion. Secondly, Prahalad suggests that traditional products, services and management processes will not work. Instead companies must learn to innovate and take into account their customers' low and irregular cash flows. For example, a pay-per-use business model will allow customers to pay low costs for each use of a product or service and therefore encourage consumption and help to increase access and choice to an increasing number of branded consumer products. Instead of assuming that the poor cannot afford certain products and services and so do not represent a viable market, the emphasis must now shift towards recognising their willingness to pay and to thinking about how to bring the benefits of global standards at affordable prices.

Finally, while much of the focus in the BOP literature has been on how individual companies can best serve the poor in developing countries, significant attention has also been given to the importance of developing an ecosystem surrounding these companies – a network or community of different organisations (for-profit, non-profit, private, state) which all play an important role in helping the company to deliver the finished product or service. Prahalad's simple message is 'don't go it alone', and he concludes by suggesting that the key stakeholders in this debate need to have a change in mindset as the dominant logic of each group is continuing to restrict their ability to see the opportunities which now exist.

While the first section of Prahalad's publication focused on explaining the rationale behind increasing private sector involvement in the fight against poverty, sections two and three showcased examples of private companies in a variety of different markets serving large numbers of low-income families. This evidence was impossible to ignore, and it quickly made any blanket condemnation of for-profit companies operating in these markets untenable. The remarkable growth of micro-finance and the use of mobile phones in developing countries have also helped to reinforce Prahalad's message that the profit motive can be harnessed to do good. Across the developing world mobile phones are now being used to communicate with distant relatives, learn English, pay bills, transfer money, access saving accounts, combat AIDS, and provide farmers with up-to-date price information. This clearly suggests that there is a demand for particular goods and services in these communities, as long as they are made affordable. These developments therefore raise an intriguing question – is it now possible to apply to education the same level of innovation, ecosystem development and focus on affordability that has occurred in other markets, including the market for mobile phones?

While Prahalad did not include an example of budget private schools as a case study in his 2004 publication, he did identify the global education industry as a BOP market which was now emerging as a major opportunity. Education remained on the periphery of the BOP debate, however, perhaps because the sector was still viewed as being too politically sensitive. This changed in 2006 when James Tooley's essay *Educating Amaretch: Private Schools for the Poor and the New Frontier for Investors* won the first prize in the International Finance Corporation (IFC) and *Financial Times*' first annual essay competition entitled 'Business and development: private path to prosperity'. Building on his research over the previous decade, Tooley recommended that the development community could assist the poor by extending access to private schools through targeted scholarships and vouchers. Private investors could also contribute through micro-finance-type loans, dedicated education investment funds and joint ventures with educational entrepreneurs, including the development of chains of budget private schools. Together with an extract from the winning essay, the *Financial Times* also published an editorial, which concludes with the following statement:

> Education is not, as has long been believed, too important to be left to the private sector. It is, instead, too important to be left to failing government monopolies. The private-sector revolution empowers the one group of people that cares about the education of children: their parents. Outsiders – both official and private – must build on the initiative the poor have shown. (*Financial Times*, 17 February 2007)

Emerging chains of budget private schools

The most exciting development to occur in this private sector revolution in education concerns the growth of a number of chains of budget private schools which have ambitious plans to expand nationally and then across the developing world. For example, Bridge International Academies (BIA)[2] was set up in Kenya in 2009 with a mission to revolutionise access to affordable, high-quality primary education for poor families across Africa. By July 2011 22 schools had been opened in the slums of Nairobi and the company now has plans rapidly to scale the company and expand across sub-Saharan Africa. By 2015 they hope to have a total of 1,800 schools serving more than one million families. To enable an expansion of this size they have introduced a 'School

2 www.bridgeinternationalacademies.com.

in a Box' model, which provides each new local school manager with a detailed step-by-step set of instructions on how to set up and manage a new school. Some of the key features of this model include the following: the time from conception to opening is five months; school buildings are constructed for less than $2,000 per classroom; parents are charged 295 Kenyan shillings ($4) per month, which is estimated to be less than the unofficial fees charged at local 'free' government schools; each school will be able to enrol up to 1,000 children and will expect to become profitable within one year of opening; students attend school each weekday from 7.30 a.m. to 5 p.m.; both school managers and teachers are employed from the local community, and while their base salaries are low they receive bonuses for increasing enrolment and the on-time payment of school fees; and finally, detailed lesson plans are developed at the head office with a particular emphasis on ensuring that children have a good understanding of English.

An important initiative introduced by BIA concerns the use of a custom-built automated, computerised student payment system, which allows parents to pay school fees using a mobile phone. This technology is also used to manage the majority of each school's financial transactions, helping to create a 'cashless school system'. The head office therefore distributes school budgets and teacher salaries by mobile money transfers and parents are also expected to pay school fees in the same way. As no money is handled within each school, teachers are restricted in the ability to demand extra payments and parents are also asked to report any demands for such payments to the head office.

To help fund its ambitious expansion plans BIA has also succeeded in attracting a significant amount of private investment from a new generation of impact investors, including: Deutsche

Bank Americas Foundation; Omidyar Network; Jasmine Social Investments; d.o.b. foundation; LGT Venture Philanthropy; Hilti Foundation; and Learn Capital. According to Matt Bannick, managing partner of Omidyar Network, BIA provides a compelling example of high-impact entrepreneurship which is 'not only extending access to education, but also serving as a model of how others can ignite social change through for-profit innovation'. Following the lead taken by these impact investors, more established companies are now beginning to take an interest, including Pearson, which became a significant minority investor in BIA in March 2011. As these school chains begin to grow and develop we should expect more national and global companies to follow Pearson's lead. BIA (a for-profit company with ambitious plans to expand) is therefore helping to attract an entirely new source of private investment into education and providing a new opportunity for private investors from around the world to make a positive contribution to the development of education in the slums of Nairobi, Kenya. According to JP Morgan, the potential size of investment in the primary education market alone over the next ten years could be $4.8–$10 billion, with an estimated profit opportunity of $2.6–$11 billion.

In Ghana, Omega Schools[3] is another new chain of budget private schools which describes itself as a for-profit business with a social mission 'to create private schools that benefit low income families and empower aspirations of those at the bottom of the income pyramid'. After the first Omega School was launched in 2009, the number of schools had increased to ten by 2011, and the company now plans to expand the chain across West Africa.

3 www.omega-schools.com.

An important innovation pioneered by Omega Schools has been the introduction of the daily fee, which accommodates the many parents that cannot afford to pay monthly or termly fees. This fee covers tuition costs, uniform, books, transport, deworming programmes and a hot meal. Each child also receives fifteen free school days a year and an insurance policy which guarantees that every child will complete their schooling in the event of the death of a parent. The popularity of the pay-per-use business model applied to schooling is highlighted by the fact that the demand for places at each new Omega School has been high, and the same model is now being introduced by a number of competing private schools in the local area. As noted on their website, Omega Schools is now looking to introduce 'rapid incremental innovations that, if successful, will not only yield benefits to our students, but will also have the potential to be widely replicated, yielding benefits to learners outside our system'. Omega Schools' innovative Pay As You Learn (PAYL) model combined with very low overheads has allowed the company to break even in 2011. These ten schools are therefore financially self-sustainable and do not depend on any external funding from governments or international agencies. This is a remarkable achievement, and it confirms that when schools are given the space and freedom to develop they can flourish without government support.

This example, therefore, helps to shed light on how the profit motive in education can help to benefit not only the children attending the school through introducing new innovations, but also children attending different schools, which may subsequently copy or imitate the same innovation. A process of continual innovation, which is normally associated with more competitive sectors of the economy, is therefore slowly beginning to emerge in these new education markets. Research published by the Monitor Institute has identified Omega Schools as an 'emerging phenomenon with high potential to counter the causes and consequences of global poverty' (Kubzansky et al., 2011: 26). Again, this is not simply referring to the potential of Omega Schools operating in complete isolation. Rather, it also takes into account the transformative effect that opening an Omega School could have on other schools operating in the local area. After the multiplier effect has been taken into account, it becomes much easier to see how an innovation introduced in one school can be quickly imitated by other local schools and eventually across an entire nation. With the increasing use of the internet, perhaps it will not be long before a new innovation can spread across the global education industry within a matter of weeks.

The cashless school and the daily payment of school fees are two innovations that are already beginning to address the issues of financial mismanagement and the lack of transparency and affordability which have plagued government education sectors in developing countries over the previous half-century. The fact that the above two companies have developed and then put into practice these two innovations in less than two years shows how entrepreneurial talent, private investment and the profit motive can have a positive impact in this sector within a relatively short period of time.

A number of chains of budget private schools have also recently emerged in India, the country which is now most closely associated with this private sector revolution in education. For example, SKS Microfinance now runs approximately 60 SKS Bodhi Academies in Andhra Pradesh which provide English medium education to 3,000 children from rural villages at a cost of 160–220 rupees per month. Education is from pre-nursery to second standard, and a 'play way method' of teaching is used in classes of no more than 25 children. An initial pilot was carried out to better understand parental needs and expectations and to examine how each school in the chain can deliver the same standard of education irrespective of differences in location and teacher quality. The company is now looking to develop a system of schools that cater for more than a million poor children from the same families who take loans from SKS. As there are now estimated to be over sixty million micro-finance clients around the world, this approach of encouraging them to invest in their children's education clearly has great potential.

Another new entrant in the Indian market is Educomp Solutions, which was founded in 1994 and has since become India's largest education software company. Its new VidyaPrabhat Schools are being built in small towns and remote areas across India, and they aim to provide affordable schooling (700 rupees per month) that will blend the latest innovations in education technology with traditional Indian knowledge and values. To optimise the use of infrastructure they will operate on a shift system with primary classes in the morning and secondary classes in the afternoon, and each school will benefit from access to Educomp's numerous software applications, including: Smartclass; Mathguru; Wizlearn; Aha!Math; EasyTech and Aha!Science. This example therefore raises the possibility of some schools leapfrogging the traditional model of schooling and instead introducing a blended style of learning which combines traditional teaching with an online virtual experience.

The above developments in this emerging sector help to shed light on some important differences between government and for-profit provision in education. Firstly, the different approaches, methods and models being introduced by these new chains suggest that the profit motive will help to encourage diversity and a variety of different models of schooling, with each model reflecting the nature of the environment in which it operates. Secondly, for-profit provision appears to be encouraging a willingness to experiment and try new things. Therefore, instead of schools looking towards the Ministry of Education for direction and inspiration, each separate company is now investing in research and development (R&D) to help continually improve how they manage their schools, use technology and deliver particular subjects. R&D will therefore become much more driven by the specific needs of each different education company. This stands in stark contrast to the vast majority of research carried out in many government education sectors, which often takes place within a university department with little or no contact with local schools. The way in which these new school chains organise and manage their R&D activities may prove to be an important factor that will help to determine whether they achieve their full potential and develop into a national or global chain.

Developing ecosystems for wealth creation in education

As previously noted by Prahalad, companies looking to enter BOP markets should not do so alone, and this applies in particular to companies looking to enter education markets in developing countries. An important player in these new ecosystems or networks in education will be organisations providing a variety of different financial services. In *Educating Amaretch*, Tooley suggested that a creative new frontier for investors was now emerging to meet the increasing demand for micro-finance services within this low-cost private education sector. This was reinforced in 2008 when Opportunity International, one of the world's largest microfinance companies, introduced its Microschools of Opportunity programme, which provides loans to education entrepreneurs and business advice on how to succeed and run a school which is financially self-sustainable. As the timely repayment of loans will depend on how each loan is spent and how successful each school becomes, Opportunity International has a clear interest in helping each school to succeed. Microschools are now operating in fifty locations in Ghana and nine in Malawi, and they intend to expand into several other countries across Africa and Asia. Opportunity International also offers school fee loans to parents, helping them to pay school fees over a period of time, which is more compatible with their irregular cash flow. School savings accounts for children are also being developed to help encourage families to save money for their children's education. All these initiatives will help children across the developing world gain access to a quality of education that national governments and international agencies have previously been unable to provide.

One organisation which is now applying the BOP approach to education is an impact investment company based in Atlanta, USA, called Gray Ghost Ventures (GGV). Recognising the potential in the rapidly expanding market for affordable private schools across India, GGV identified financing as one of the key barriers to growth within the sector. To address this need, in 2009 they established the Indian School Finance Company (ISFC), which provides loans at market rates to low-cost private schools operating in Hyderabad, Andhra Pradesh. Loans are targeted at expanding school infrastructure and capacity and are combined with a management training programme for school owners. This allows the school to increase enrolment, which increases school revenue and therefore improves the school's ability to repay the loan. To complement the provision of these financial services, GGV's charitable arm is also looking to help ensure that these schools offer quality education in a sustainable manner. Its Affordable Private School Initiative includes the development of a rating and accreditation system; research into the nature and extent of the affordable private school markets in India, Africa and South America; and the launch of its EnterprisingSchools.com website. The development of new rating and accreditation systems and a new generation of branded qualifications are two important areas which this emerging sector will need to address, otherwise governments are likely to intervene.

This initiative therefore represents a new development in charitable giving, whereby funds are used to help develop a new market, improve the way it works and make it more attractive to potential private investors. If these charitable investments can help to kick-start a new industry then they clearly have the potential to have a much greater long-term impact than a traditional charitable donation, which may be focused only on providing an immediate and short-term impact. This use of charitable funds also corresponds with Prahalad's insistence that, where government subsidies, international aid and charitable donations are to be used, then 'our goal should be to build capacity for people to escape poverty and deprivation through self-sustaining market-based systems' (Prahalad, 2004: 8).

Another example of how a charity can help to support a self-sustainable market-based system in education can be found in the slums of Nairobi, where Scholarships for Kids (SFK) has introduced the first scholarship programme dedicated to helping children gain access to a local fee-paying private school. SFK has designed a model addressing many of the issues which continue to undermine donor confidence in traditional development projects, including the lack of transparency, the misappropriation of funds, and money failing to reach those most in need. For example, schools chosen to be included in the scheme must maintain certain standards and scholarship children must maintain an excellent attendance record or the scholarship is withdrawn. In order to encourage participating schools to be self-sufficient, SFK also has a policy that permits no more than 15 per cent of school places to be funded by its scholarships, which helps to protect the long-term sustainability of each private school. As a result, because the greater part of the school's income will still come from fee-paying parents, the school will still be expected to be competitive with other schools and provide value for money. It is this self-reinforcing mechanism which will hopefully guarantee that those children who receive a scholarship will receive a valuable educational experience. SFK is now in a position to provide potential donors with a cost-effective and accountable service, which guarantees that their donations will be used to fund the education of those children most in need without undermining the sustainability of each private school.

It is clear that the growth and development of these networks of different organisations, from micro-finance companies to scholarship charities, are going to play a critical role in helping education companies develop and manage large chains of private schools. This suggests that any discussion about the potential role of the profit motive in education must also take into account the important role being played by these supporting organisations, including non-profit charities and foundations.

The United Nations and the profit motive in education

In addition to helping to challenge the political consensus in international development, C. K. Prahalad also played an important role in helping to encourage a number of UN agencies to embrace a much more pro-business approach in their fight against global poverty. In July 2003 Prahalad joined the United Nations Development Programme (UNDP) Commission on the Private Sector and Development, which examined how private sector entrepreneurship can best be unleashed in developing countries. The Commission's 2004 report, *Unleashing Entrepreneurship: Making Business Work for the Poor,* found that while the private sector was already meeting the needs of the poor in places that were difficult to reach, it was also clear that entrepreneurs in developing countries often faced significant regulatory and licensing hurdles. The report concluded by calling for fresh thinking about international development unconstrained by ideology and unhinged from previous counterproductive debates about the government sector versus the private sector. Instead, the core message was simple – the Millennium Development Goals (MDGs), including guaranteeing universal access to primary education, will not be achieved without engaging the private sector and unleashing the power of entrepreneurship.

Building on the success of this report, the UNDP launched its Growing Inclusive Markets (GIM) initiative[4] in 2006 to help demonstrate how doing business with the poor can be mutually beneficial.[5] Its first report, *Creating Value for All: Strategies for Doing*

4 www.growinginclusivemarkets.org.

5 Numerous different initiatives have been introduced to help support, document and encourage the growth and development of inclusive business models, including: the International Finance Corporation's (IFC) Inclusive Business Group (www.ifc.org/ifcext/advisoryservices.nsf/Content/BOP_Inclusive_Business);

Business with the Poor (UNDP, 2008), identified 50 successful businesses across the developing world that generated a profit while also achieving a positive social impact. Also introduced was the concept of an inclusive business model which includes 'the poor on the demand side as clients and customers, and on the supply side as employees, producers and business owners at various points in the value chain. They build bridges between business and the poor for mutual benefit' (ibid.: 2). The link between expanding private sector involvement in education and reducing poverty and promoting human development was also reinforced – poverty being defined 'not simply as a lack of income, but more fundamentally as a lack of meaningful choices' and the basic purpose of development as 'to enlarge people's choices' (ibid.: 20).

In its second global report, *The MDG's: Everyone's Business* (Gradl et al., 2010), the importance of for-profit companies is again reinforced, this time in relation to achieving the MDGs, including guaranteeing universal access to primary education. Quoting research published by Tooley and Dixon (2005), the report confirms that private education has expanded dramatically over the last two decades, and that in some low-income areas in India and Africa the majority of schoolchildren are now enrolled in private schools. Private companies are therefore encouraged to '[p]rovide affordable, high-quality education by running schools in slums and rural areas' (Gradl et al., 2010: 24). This will allow companies to use their specific processes to promote innovation and therefore act as a 'conveyor belt for innovative solutions'.

WBCSD-SNV Inclusive Business Alliance (www.inclusivebusiness.org); International Leaders Business Forum (ILBF) Inclusive Growth Programme (www.iblf.org/en/programmes/Inclusive-Growth.aspx); and Monitor Group Inclusive Markets initiative (www.mim.monitor.com).

Furthermore, increasing private sector involvement in the delivery of education will mean that successful approaches can be replicated in different countries instead of being confined to one geographical area. This is an important benefit of increasing private sector involvement in the delivery of education which is seldom discussed in the literature.

The United Nations has also introduced a number of pro-business initiatives, including Business Call to Action (BCtA) and 'Business.un.org' – a website which allows companies to identify partnership opportunities and submit ideas for collaboration. A common theme which links all of these different initiatives is the concept of the inclusive business model, which acknowledges the ability of for-profit companies to serve low-income communities, while at the same time generating profit. According to the WBCSD–SNV Inclusive Business Alliance, 'an inclusive business is an economically profitable, environmentally and socially responsible entrepreneurial initiative, which integrates low-income communities in its value chain for the mutual benefit of both the company and the community. It seeks to improve the livelihoods of low-income populations while increasing returns to the company' (2011: 12). For example, the International Finance Corporation (IFC) has recently documented the growth of the 'Value for Money Degrees' model, which makes university education accessible to all through a combination of innovations that increase affordability and value. An example is Anhanguera in Brazil, which educates 650,000 students a year on its campuses and 100,000 students online (Jenkins et al., 2011). The Monitor Institute has documented the 'Private Vocational Training at the Seam' model, which enables private vocational colleges to provide low-cost, no-frills, quality further education courses. In South

Africa more than seven hundred private colleges currently provide learning opportunities for over 700,000 students (Kubzansky et al., 2011: 75–87).

These policy developments within the UN and the wider development community therefore represent a significant change in direction for an international agency that has traditionally looked to national governments to finance and deliver education. The world of business was either largely ignored or seen as part of the problem. For example, writing in 2009, Prahalad states that '[u]ntil recently, little attention was paid to the role of the private sector in poverty alleviation. The Millennium Development Goals were originally developed without recognition of the role that the private sector could play' (Prahalad, 2009: 5). With the benefit of hindsight this is a remarkable statement, as it suggests that the greater part of the international community had previously been attempting to 'make poverty history' without taking into account the role of the private sector, an approach still being used at the turn of the millennium. The timing of this change in direction by the UN is also referred to in a report published by the UN Global Compact Office, which states that direct cooperation between the private sector and the UN emerged in the late 1990s in response to 'the complexity of global problems, the scarcity of resources and the failure of multilateral mechanisms to address these issues' (United Nations Global Compact Office, 2010: 6). It is perhaps ironic that the UN had previously justified increasing levels of government planning because of the increasing complexity of global problems. Today, it is this same complexity which is now making central government planning redundant.

Finally, it is also important to recognise that the UN is not alone in recognising the potential of for-profit companies to transform the way education is provided to those living at the bottom of the pyramid. In recent years the World Bank, USAID and DfID have all updated and adapted their strategies on education to take into account the recent growth in private sector provision. The burgeoning of a new impact investment community in the last few years also suggests that there are now an increasing number of philanthropic foundations and venture capitalists who are beginning to invest in BOP markets around the world, including education. Vinod Khosla, the Indian-born billionaire and co-founder of Sun Microsystems, is a good example of someone who now invests in companies that profit the poor and still generate a profit themselves. According to Khosla, while the intentions of governments, international agencies and non-profit charities are not being challenged, their ability to get things done in a sustainable way certainly is. He now plans to start a venture capital fund to invest in companies that focus on the poor in India and Africa by providing services such as health and education.

The need for new thinking has also been recognised by Bill Gates, who has previously championed the concept of 'creative capitalism', which he has described as 'an approach where governments, businesses, and non-profits work together to stretch the reach of market forces so that more people can make a profit, or gain recognition, doing work that eases the world's inequities' (Gates, 2008). And it is not just business leaders who are beginning to challenge the consensus. For example, according to Pope Benedict XVI, the traditional distinction between for-profits and non-profits can no longer do full justice to reality or offer practical direction for the future. After recognising the growth in the number of businesses with an explicitly social mission, the Pope concludes:

> This is not merely a matter of a 'third sector', but of a broad new composite reality embracing the private and government spheres, one which does not exclude profit, but instead considers it a means for achieving human and social ends. Whether such companies distribute dividends or not, whether their juridical structure corresponds to one or other of the established forms, becomes secondary in relation to their willingness to view profit as a means of achieving the goal of a more humane market and society. (Pope Benedict XVI, *Caritas in veritate*, 2009)

This approach also corresponds with the thoughts of Jim Fruchterman, a veteran social entrepreneur in the USA, who believes that '[s]electing a legal structure is not a question of moral purity. I am structure agnostic: I believe that for-profit and non-profit structures can both be good vehicles for improving society' (Fruchterman, 2011).

Lessons for the UK

The growth and development of a number of pioneering chains of private schools serving low-income communities across the developing world is a fascinating development which is part of a much broader trend towards using the power of the profit motive and entrepreneurship to help serve the basic needs of the poor. As noted above, for the UN the key lesson was simple – the Millennium Development Goals (including guaranteeing universal access to primary education) will not be achieved without engaging the private sector and unleashing the power of entrepreneurship. When applied to the UK the key lesson is also simple – a world-class education system will not be achieved without engaging the private sector and unleashing the power of entrepreneurship.

For those frustrated by the lack of progress in developing an open and diverse education sector in the UK, these developments in the UN may provide some hope. Firstly, they show that bold changes in education policy are possible within a relatively short period of time. Future changes in UN policy should also be expected as the state-versus-private debate becomes increasingly irrelevant. This may involve an increasing focus on the users of education and how best to empower parents and students to make their own informed decisions. Secondly, these developments also show that the UK government is now lagging behind the UN in terms of its willingness to make the reforms required to help create an open and diverse education sector fit for the 21st century. It is also important to note that, owing to the size and nature of the organisation, UN policy does not necessarily represent international best practice. Instead, it often lags behind the latest developments and initiatives in the field. UN policy should therefore be viewed as an absolute minimum, which suggests that, if the UK simply wants to maintain its current global rankings, then gradual or piecemeal reform will no longer be sufficient.

Obviously, there are significant differences between an unelected international agency and an elected coalition government with one eye on the next election. That said, the UN can also be described as a coalition of different partners, many of which have previously been openly hostile to increasing private sector involvement in education. It is therefore worth taking note of the strategies and arguments used by the UN to present its case for change.

Most notably, it was not UNESCO, the UN agency responsible

for education, which was the driving force behind the inclusive business agenda. Instead, the United Nations Development Programme (UNDP) took the lead as part of its wider remit to promote private sector growth in developing countries. Also, the UNDP did not act alone. Rather it either worked with or was supported by a number of global think tanks, academic research centres and international organisations, including the World Resources Institute and the World Economic Forum. Furthermore, although the UNDP did not directly target education, the general case for the use of inclusive business models in other sectors was made and then, when accepted, it was extended into education. This whole approach was pragmatic – calls were made for decision-makers to focus on outcomes and not be ideological: institutions that improved outcomes were therefore deemed desirable regardless of whether they were government or private. Finally, perhaps the most significant aspect of the UN's change in policy concerned the terminology used to help ensure that it received widespread support and also make it much more difficult for the sceptics to argue against the change in policy. The use of the word 'inclusive' is central to this strategy, describing a particular business model used by companies operating in BOP markets. The word can also be used to describe the education sector as a whole, a more inclusive education sector referring to one which does not discriminate against or exclude schools simply because of their legal and organisational structure. Education sectors are also increasingly being referred to as 'open' (as opposed to closed) and 'diverse' (as opposed to uniform), which again critics often find difficult to argue against. A UK government looking to follow the UN's lead must therefore not underestimate the importance of language in this debate.

References

Bucheli, M. (2009), *Inclusive Business: A New Strategic Paradigm at the Bottom of the Pyramid Markets: A case study analysis*, St Gallen: Arbeit University.

Fruchterman, J. (2011), 'For love or lucre', *Stanford Social Innovation Review*, Spring, pp. 42–7.

Gates, B. (2008), 'A new approach to capitalism in the 21st century', World Economic Forum, Davos, Switzerland, 24 January.

Gradl, C., S. Sivakumaran and S. Sobhani (2010), *The MDG's: Everyone's Business*, New York: United Nations Development Programme.

Jenkins, B., E. Ishikawa, A. Geaneotes, P. Baptista and T. Masuoka (2011), *Accelerating Inclusive Business Opportunities: Business Models that Make a Difference*, Washington, DC: International Finance Corporation.

Kandachar, P. and M. Halme (2008), *Sustainability Challenges and Solutions at the Base of the Pyramid: Business, Technology and the Poor*, Sheffield: Greenleaf Publishing.

Kubzansky, M., A. Cooper and V. Barbary (2011), *Promise and Progress: Market-based Solutions to Poverty in Africa*, Cambridge, MA: Monitor Institute.

London, T. and S. Hart (2010), *Next Generation Business Strategies for the Base of the Pyramid*, London: Financial Times/Prentice Hall.

Prahalad, C. K. (2004), *The Fortune at the Bottom of the Pyramid: Eradicating Poverty through Profits*, Upper Saddle River, NJ: Wharton School Publishing.

Prahalad, C. K. (2009), *The Fortune at the Bottom of the Pyramid: Eradicating Poverty through Profits*, new edn, Upper Saddle River, NJ: Wharton School Publishing.

Tooley, J. (1999), *The Global Education Industry – Lessons from Private Education in Developing Countries*, Hobart Paper 141, London: Institute of Economic Affairs.

Tooley, J. (2006), *Educating Amaretch: Private Schools for the Poor and the New Frontier for Investors*, London: Financial Times and International Finance Corporation.

Tooley, J. (2009), *The Beautiful Tree, a Personal Journey into How the World's Poorest People Are Educating Themselves*, Washington, DC: Cato Institute.

Tooley, J. and P. Dixon (2005), *Private Education Is Good for the Poor: A Study of Private Schools Serving the Poor in Low-income Countries*, Washington, DC: Cato Institute.

UNDP (United Nations Development Programme) (2008), *Creating Value for All: Strategies for Doing Business with the Poor*, New York: United Nations.

United Nations Global Compact Office (2010), *UN–Private Sector Collaboration since 2000*, New York: United Nations.

WBCSD–SNV (World Business Council for Sustainable Development and Netherlands Development Organisation (2011), *Inclusive Business – Creating Value in Latin America*, The Hague: Alliance for Inclusive Business.

Wilson, C. and P. Wilson (2006), *Make Poverty Business: Increase Profits and Reduce Risk by Engaging with the Poor*, Sheffield: Greenleaf Publishing.

7 FOR-PROFIT HIGHER EDUCATION IN THE UNITED STATES

Daniel L. Bennett, Adam R. Lucchesi and Richard K. Vedder

For-profit post-secondary education in the USA has historically been limited to independently owned schools offering vocationally oriented training, while state and private non-profit colleges have managed to capture the title 'traditional' higher education. That is slowly beginning to change as private capital and entrepreneurship are changing the higher education landscape. Many for-profit firms have adopted a mass-market corporate approach that has permitted them to begin competing directly with the state and private non-profit institutions for students and resources. This contemporary phenomenon has enabled the for-profit sector to experience remarkable growth and success over the past several decades.

Growth of for-profit higher education

Between 1986 and 2008, enrolment in the for-profit sector grew from around 300,000 to more than 1.8 million students, an annual growth rate of 8.4 per cent, far outpacing growth rates of 1.5 per cent in both the state and private non-profit sectors.[1] This divergence

1 Cellini and Goldin (2012) estimate that current enrolment at profit-seeking institutions is 2.5 million, accounting for students attending institutions that do not participate in federal financial aid programmes and are not included in government statistics.

Figure 1 **For-profit autumn enrolment by institution level, 1986–2008**

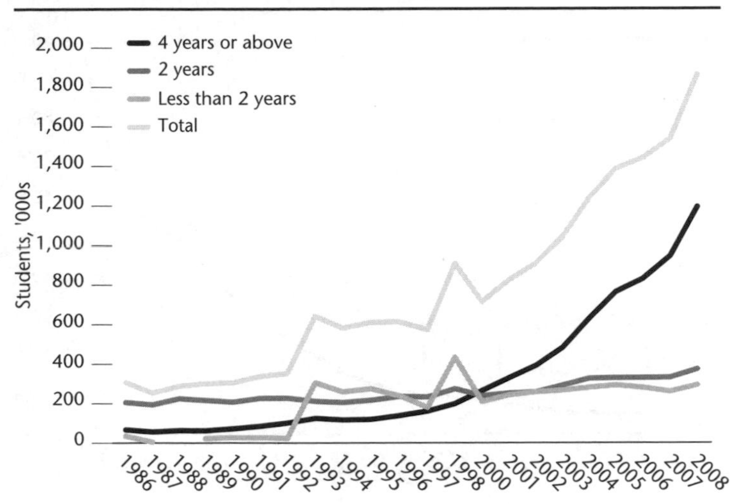

Source: US Department of Education, NCES, IPEDS, authors' calculations

in growth rates has permitted the for-profit sector to increase its market share nearly fourfold during the period: from 2.4 per cent in 1986 to 9.2 per cent in 2008. Figure 1 shows the growth in for-profit autumn enrolment by institution level between 1986 and 2008.

Between 1986 and 1998, growth among the for-profits occurred mainly for courses that are for less than two years, indicative of the sector's traditional focus on vocational education. Enrolment in this segment of the market grew at an average annual rate of 21.6 per cent during this twelve-year period, raising the sector's share of the less-than-two-year market from 21.3 to 78.9 per cent. The for-profits share of this market has remained relatively constant since 1998. The real engine of growth in the for-profit

Figure 2 **For-profit market share by institution level, 1986–2008**

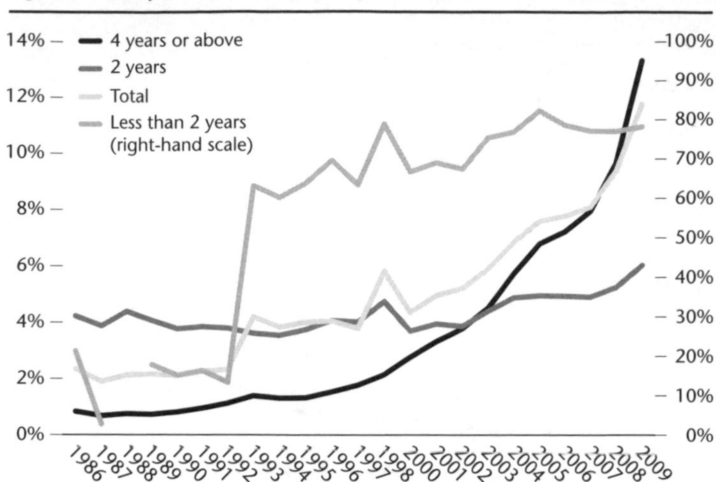

Notes: Less-than-two-year market share plotted on the right-hand axis; 1988 enrolment data not available.
Source: US Department of Education, NCES, IPEDS, authors' calculations

sector over the past two decades, and especially during the most recent decade, has been among institutions providing courses of four years or longer. Since 1986, enrolment at such for-profit institutions has grown at an average annual rate of 13.4 per cent, with enrolment growing at 17.7 per cent since 1998. Enrolment growth at government and non-profit institutions providing four-year courses has been much more modest, with the former increasing enrolment at an annual rate of 1.4 per cent and the latter at 1.7 per cent per annum, since 1986. These growth trends have permitted the for-profit sector to increase its share of the four-year market from less than 1 per cent in 1986 to nearly 10 per cent in 2008. Early indicators suggest that the for-profits captured well above

10 per cent of the four-year market in 2009. Figure 2 shows the growth in market share of for-profit schools by institutional level from 1986 to 2009.

Much of the sector's growth can be attributed to generous federal financial aid policies that have not only accelerated the demand for higher education at a rate much faster than government and private non-profit colleges have been able to absorb, but which have also attracted investment from the private capital markets. Total federal outlays for student financial assistance reached nearly $117 billion in 2008/09. In 1986/87, this figure was less than $30 billion (in constant 2008 dollars), representing an inflation-adjusted annual growth rate of 6.4 per cent over the time period. Since 1990/91, the annual growth rate in federal outlays has been even greater at 7.2 per cent, with the average total federal aid per full-time equivalent (FTE) student more than doubling from an inflation-adjusted $5,093 in 1990/91 to $11,842 in 2008/09.

The tremendous growth of federal student aid spurred an increase in demand for post-secondary education, providing many individuals who may have been previously deterred from higher education with a means to pay for it. The for-profit sector has proved incredibly adept at serving the new wave of students and attracting the federal money following them. This includes students of non-traditional college age, minorities and those from lower socio-economic backgrounds, all of whom continue to remain largely underserved by the traditional higher education system.

In fact, more than half of students enrolled at for-profit institutions in 2007 were above 25 years of age, while only one quarter to one third of students attending private non-profit and government colleges were 25 years or older. Minorities also make up a larger share of for-profit enrolments than at government and private non-profit colleges, as black, Hispanic, Asian and American Indian students comprise nearly 40 per cent of total for-profit enrolments, whereas the same groups accounted for only 31 per cent and 25 per cent of enrolments in government and private non-profit institutions, respectively. Female students also account for a larger share of for-profit enrolments than at traditional institutions, making up 64 per cent of total for-profit enrolments: females accounted for 57 and 58 per cent of enrolments at government and private non-profit colleges, respectively.

For-profit students are also generally from lower socio-economic backgrounds than students at traditional colleges. According to an analysis by the Government Accountability Office, the annual median family income of for-profit students was 60 and 49 per cent of that of students attending government and private non-profit colleges, respectively, in 2004. They were also far more likely to be first-generation college students, as only 37 per cent of for-profit students reported having a parent with an associate's degree or higher, while 52 and 61 per cent of government and private non-profit students, respectively, reported the same. For-profit students are also likely to receive less family financial support, as 76 per cent were classified as financially dependent in 2007/08 versus 50 and 39 per cent of students in the government and private non-profit sectors, respectively.

For-profit institutions are subject to significant political risk

The sector's success in enrolling historically underserved students

Figure 3 **Percentage of Pell Grant and Stafford Loans dollars captured by the for-profit sector**

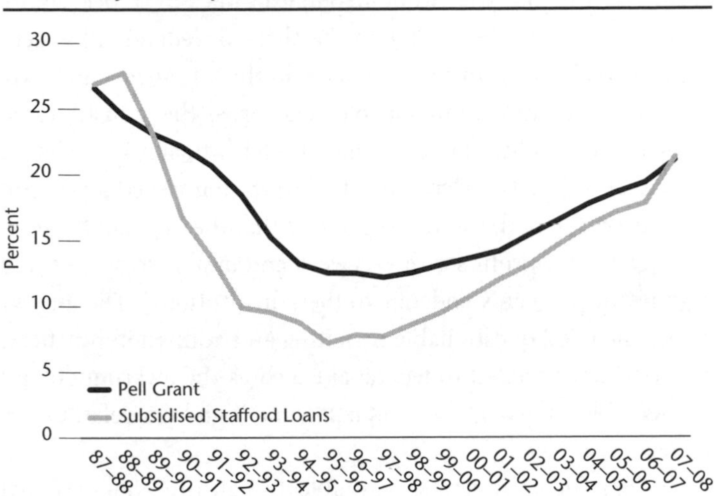

Source: The College Board, 'Trends in Financial Aid 2009'

has enabled it to achieve a growing market share and capture an increasing portion of federal aid dollars. In fact, 21 per cent of all federal Pell Grant and subsidised Stafford Loan expenditures were used at for-profit institutions in 2007/08. These figures grew from 12.2 and 7.7 per cent of expenditures, respectively, in 1997/98. The share of federal aid dollars landing at for-profit institutions, however, is lower now than it was in 1987/88, as depicted in Figure 3. Success on the part of for-profit colleges in attracting federal student aid has often been accompanied by political ramifications.

The trends indicated above are largely reflective of a dynamic political environment in which Democratic legislatures and presidential administrations have exhibited a tendency to be hostile to the industry, while Republican ones have been more accommodating. The decline in the share of federal aid expenditures received by for-profit colleges in the late 1980s and early 1990s was largely attributable to this factor, as the industry came under serious political attack similar to that which is being levied against it today. The Department of Education issued a series of reports critical of the sector, suggesting that the 'regulatory structure for the for-profit sector was weak and unable to address the significant problems endemic to these institutions'. The alleged issues included questionable recruiting and admission practices, and problems related to federal aid such as the awarding of aid to ineligible students, low completion and high loan default rates (Kinser, 2006).

When the Democrats were able to capture congressional majorities in the late 1980s, they began work on crafting regulations that would significantly curtail the ability of for-profit institutions to compete. The first round of regulations was included in the Omnibus Budget Reconciliation Act of 1990, which would terminate institutions with unacceptably high default rates from participation in the federal loan programme. Further regulations were introduced in the 1992 Higher Education Act (HEA), which included a rule stipulating that no more than 85 per cent of a for-profit school's revenue could come from federal student aid (the 85/15 rule), as well as a number of other measures, such as a limit on the use of distance education and a ban on the use of incentive compensation for admissions officials.

The cumulative effects of the new regulatory rules on the for-profit industry were significant and almost immediate, as many profit-seeking schools were unable to comply and closed. In fact, the number of for-profit schools accredited by one of the six major national accrediting agencies declined by 5.1 per cent the year after the 1992 HEA, and by 13.9 per cent by 1995. In addition, the for-profit sector's share of federal aid dollars declined in the wake of the legislation, as can be seen in Figure 3. The rules did, however, have a positive impact on student loan default rates in the for-profit sector, as they declined from 36 to 24 per cent between 1991 and 1993 (Moore, 1995).

This suggests that the sector's reliance on federal aid money exposed it to political risk and regulatory authority that significantly reined in its growth. The growth resumed, however, in the mid-1990s as Republicans regained control of Congress. The 1998 HEA reauthorisation would liberalise some of the earlier regulations. Major changes included a softening of the 85/15 rule to allow institutions to receive up to 90 per cent of their revenues from federal aid programmes and expanded access to federal aid programmes for distance learners. The loosening of regulation in the late 1990s allowed the for-profit industry to once again resume its earlier growth, as can be seen in Figure 1 above.

The sector's success has once again come under political attack, as Congressional Democrats and the Obama administration have exhibited rigorous hostility towards for-profit higher education in an attempt to stringently regulate the industry. The reasoning espoused by the current politicians is very similar to that used to rein in the sector two decades ago, as allegations of abusive recruitment practices, misleading advertising and questionable educational value are cited along with growing student loan default rates in the sector as an imperative to impose onerous new regulations. The regulations enacted thus far include stricter rules concerning student loan defaults, barring of employee incentive compensation, enhanced data reporting requirements and, most controversially, changes to a rule known as gainful employment. As originally proposed, the new gainful employment regulation would have imposed a severely flawed programme-level debt-to-expected-income metric, with programmes failing to meet specific criteria losing eligibility for federal financial aid programmes.

In the US higher education system, losing federal aid eligibility is considered to be the kiss of death for an institution. Most analyses of the gainful employment proposal reached the conclusion that the rule would have had a significant impact on the sector: displacing hundreds of thousands of students, limiting the types of educational programmes offered, and hampering the ability of private enterprises to set their own prices.[2] The for-profit sector was acutely aware of the potentially devastating effect of the rule change as it lobbied extensively in opposition to gainful employment. Its lobbying efforts were fruitful to some extent, as the final rules released in June 2011 were softened from the initial proposal.

Despite much valid criticism about gainful employment and isolation of the for-profit sector for enhanced regulatory control, the Obama Administration and its allies seem intent on imposing further intrusive regulations intended to impede the ability of for-profit higher education to compete fairly. The latest efforts include proposals to lower the maximum share of revenues that a school can generate from federal financial aid from 90 to 85 per cent, and adding veteran education benefits, which are currently exempt, to this calculation.

The *Wall Street Journal* concluded that the Obama

2 Cf. Bennett et al. (2010); Brinner (2010); Guryan and Thompson (2010); Kantrowitz (2010); Miller (2010).

administration's 'hostility to private education companies ... is consistent with [its] decision to bar private companies from delivering student loans, its near-takeover of the health-care industry, and its denunciations of high business pay and profits. By punishing for-profit colleges, the Administration will push more students into their non-profit competitors, which satisfies its preference for ... more government control.'[3] We largely agree with this assessment; as one of us argued in the *Chronicle of Higher Education*, the president's battle with for-profit higher education is part of a 'bigger war against capitalism ... that is largely ideologically based and manifestly unfair',[4] suggesting that although there are problems of fraud and abuse in the sector that need to be eradicated, a 'large portion – indeed probably a sizable majority – of the educational malpractice going on in American higher education is occurring at the not-for-profit schools so richly subsidized by the taxpayers'.[5]

Success of for-profit higher education

Political opponents and other naysayers fail to understand why the for-profit sector in the USA, which is at a competitive disadvantage in terms of tax status and a lack of institutional subsidies, continues to grow while the traditional sectors have remained relatively stagnant. They often brush aside the success of profit-seeking institutions, suggesting it is a product of corporate greed, disregard for students, misleading advertising or malicious

3 'Scapegoating For-Profit Colleges', *Wall Street Journal*, 27 August 2010.

4 Richard Vedder, 'Is Obama at War with For-Profit Universities?', *The Chronicle of Higher Education*, 30 August 2010.

5 Ibid.

conduct, neglecting the fact that the profit motive in a private enterprise system often generates competition and innovation that direct resources to productive uses and improve the general welfare of society. The consequences of private enterprise in general are that it can produce remarkable wealth for corporations and entrepreneurs that take financial risks to pursue new projects, and that decisions about the allocation of scarce resources are decided by the market. The same can be said of for-profit higher education, which has been tremendously successful financially over the past decade and a half. Although for-profit institutions do receive a sizeable portion of their revenues from federal financial aid programmes, they have to compete with the government and non-profit sectors to enrol students in order to capture this money.

Fifteen for-profit institutions comprised nearly 60 per cent of the total for-profit enrolment in 2008/09, with the Apollo Group (parent company of the University of Phoenix) alone accounting for more than 21 per cent of the market. This indicates that the for-profit higher education market exhibits a sizeable amount of market concentration among its biggest firms. This has enabled the sector to pursue a mass-market strategy and take advantage of economies of scale in the provision of educational services. To illustrate the success of for-profit higher education, we developed a For-Profit Higher Education Index (FPHI) comprising the twelve largest (by market capitalisation) publicly traded for-profit education companies in the USA. We evaluated the quarterly performance of the FPHI against that of the S&P 500 Index from June 1996 to June 2010. As Figure 4 reveals, the value of the FPHI increased by nearly 700 per cent during this period, while the value of the S&P 500 grew by only around 50 per cent.

Some observers contend that profit has absolutely no place in

Figure 4 **Center for College Affordability and Productivity For-Profit Higher Education Index**

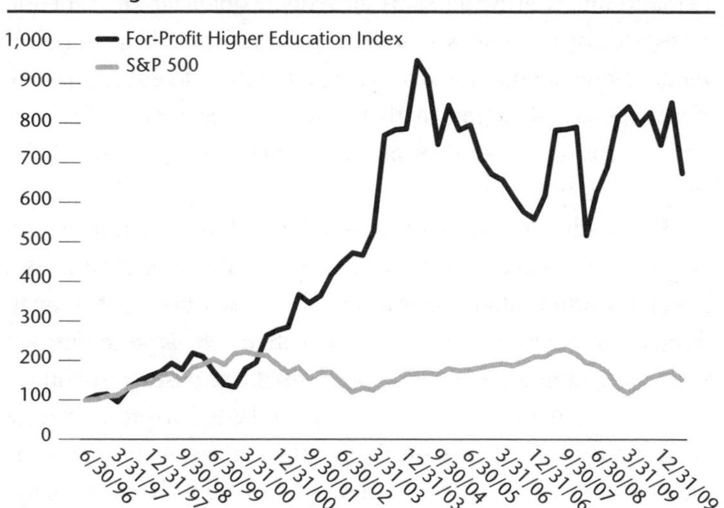

Source: Yahoo! Finance; authors' calculations

the endeavour of education and argue that for-profit colleges are akin to snake oil salesmen that do nothing more than sell students the notion that all their problems can be solved through receipt of a diploma (sometimes reflecting a dubious amount of true education), and ultimately leave them with nothing of value and a mountain of debt. Ultimately, this sort of argument – expressed in a more sophisticated way – is at the root of the political critiques.

While there is likely a small element of truth in this broad negative generalisation in an industry that is heavily subsidised by taxpayer money, our research, which includes interviews with a number of industry executives, suggests that private for-profit higher education has been successful in capturing increased demand and a growing share of federal financial aid expenditures because it employs a model that is motivated by profit. This model requires a mission that is substantially different from traditional higher education in that it requires economic efficiency and a focus on the student as a customer in order to maximise long-run profits.

For-profit education firms employ a business model that requires cost-effective resource use to remain competitive. As a result, for-profits often run less capital- and labour-intensive operations than traditional colleges, which often own large amounts of real estate to house sprawling residential campuses and employ a greater number of employees per student. For-profit institutions, on the other hand, own very little real estate, often leasing classroom space in office buildings. We asked several industry executives, 'Why do you rent most of the space you use, instead of own it?' One response was the one we expected: 'We are experts in the education business, not the real estate business'. Another was: 'In this environment with vast vacancy in commercial office space, it is possible to get real value by renting, conserving our capital'. Still a third response emphasised flexibility – if you own buildings you have a vast fixed cost, which is reduced dramatically with short-to-medium-length lease agreements. Rental allows schools to respond with respect to their space needs more quickly when student demand changes, in terms of both location and the subjects that they want taught.

Another significant operational difference between for-profit and traditional institutions is in the use of human resources. Government and non-profit institutions generally employ a greater number of staff per student than for-profit colleges.

Federally reported staff data indicate that the for-profit industry employed around 11.5 FTE staff per 100 FTE students, while government and private non-profit institutions employed approximately 18.7 and 27.4 FTE staff per 100 FTE students in 2007/08, respectively (Bennett, 2009). The disparity occurs primarily because for-profits tend to employ a lower number of non-instructional staff per student than traditional colleges do, and they require greater teaching loads from staff with virtually no research component for instructional faculty (Ruch, 2001).

For-profits also take advantage of economies of scale through practices such as employing curriculum specialists to standardise coursework across sections and campuses and by offering most courses either entirely online or by providing online supplementation. Standardised curricula allow instructors to reduce the amount of time spent on course preparation and increase the amount of time spent on teaching and meeting students. Online instruction can be offered at a low marginal cost and provides institutions with the ability to offer greater schedule flexibility and serve a greater number of prospective students. Although online education has been criticised by many as being inferior to the classroom, most research shows that online instruction is as effective, if not more effective, than traditional face-to-face instruction (cf. Means et al., 2009; Twigg, 2005). These cost-effective methods have proved to be highly profitable and are often used to subsidise brick-and-mortar campus operations, which some industry insiders contend provide tremendous marketing value that can increase the perceived legitimacy of an institution.

In addition to using a business model based on efficiency, for-profit colleges differ from traditional ones in terms of their treatment of students as customers. While traditional universities generally get only a fraction of their funding from students, nearly all revenues in for-profit education are derived from tuition charges. This suggests that for-profit institutions must be attentive to the needs of their students and treat them as valuable, paying customers. One manner in which they have been successful in doing so is by offering career-focused certificate and degree programmes, such as information technology, medical services and business management, which have measurable skills outcomes and can be completed in less time than traditional associate and bachelor degree programmes (Turner, 2006). For-profit operations also provide much greater flexibility for prospective students via evening and weekend courses held at convenient locations, in addition to online courses that can be completed remotely at the convenience of the student. Such innovations have enabled for-profit schools to appeal to many non-traditional students, as well as a growing number of traditional college-age ones, and hence to earn a reasonable return on investment.

Although many believe that improved educational outcomes can result only from increased levels of expenditure by institutions, this is a misperception that many in the education community have long exploited to gain access to additional government funds. For-profit colleges, using a lean and efficient business model, have been able to produce similar and in some cases better outcomes in terms of retention and graduation rates, especially when it comes to at-risk students (Watson, 2009), often delivering 'superior income gains ... at a societal cost comparable' with government institutions (Lytle, 2010). In doing so, they have been able to earn attractive rates of return for their investors.

Lessons for the UK

For-profit higher education in the USA has proliferated in recent decades by capturing a significant share of the growing demand for post-secondary education. While this increased demand is at least partially attributable to generous federal financial aid policies, it is undeniable that the for-profit sector has proved incredibly proficient at expanding capacity and competing with the traditional higher education sectors by offering career-oriented and vocational programmes that are in high demand. It has been able to do so in large part because it is driven by a profit motive that has proved effective and has attracted resources from the capital markets. This is in sharp contrast to the government sector, which is largely dependent on non-competitive taxpayer subsidies that have been used to finance lavish university spending that is no longer economically sustainable. The USA is not alone in facing a serious challenge in financing the growing demand for post-secondary education, as countries around the world, including the UK, face a similar reality in an age of competing demands for scarce taxpayer resources.

Students in the UK have long enjoyed very low out-of-pocket tuition charges owing to generous government subsidies that totalled £14.3 billion in 2007/08. This model of financing higher education, however, much like that in the USA, is economically unsustainable. UK policymakers recognise this. Evidence is provided by their growing willingness to allow colleges to charge higher undergraduate tuition fees, as well as imposing what is, in effect, a graduate tax on students through a loans system which will take a portion of students' earnings but be forgiving of tuition fee debts for those students with low earnings. While we are of the opinion that students derive a significant share of the benefits of higher education and should bear at least a proportional share of its cost, new government finance schemes such as a post-enrolment tax are likely not to lead to innovation or gains in efficiency. Rather, they will provide an alternative means of sustaining the status quo in higher education. More radical reforms are needed to rein in the growing costs of higher education which are primarily supported by government-imposed wealth transfers. One element of that reform is moving towards more efficient, market-based service providers, such as for-profit institutions that offer career-oriented education programmes.

These reforms should make efficiency and innovation more likely in a higher education industry that has long avoided the competitive pressures of market forces. Part of this solution involves incentivising the creation of new, privately owned or privately financed institutions by reducing existing barriers to entry and the amount of bureaucratic red tape required for a start-up. In addition, the privatisation of financially struggling institutions should be encouraged. Policies that inhibit such actions serve as protectionist measures that favour special interests, help preserve the status quo, and deflect the power of creative destruction to direct resources into productive uses and improve the general welfare of society. In addition, they impose unnecessary costs and inefficiency in an increasingly important part of the economy.

Government policy should also create a level playing field that avoids favouring some institutions at the expense of others. One policy that can help promote this is the elimination of direct institutional subsidies in favour of a voucher-style programme that students can use at their choice of institution, including those operated for a profit or offering vocational training programmes.

Economists such as the late Nobel laureate Milton Friedman have long espoused the benefits of educational vouchers in creating a more efficient and better-quality education system by providing students with the power to vote with their feet regarding the institution that deserves their resources. In the long run, however, given the essentially private nature of most educational benefits, it is preferable that most government subsidies for higher education be eliminated, with those provided to well-qualified students with financial need being the only exception. Doing so would create a more efficient and well-functioning market for higher education than is currently the case, and would lead to some of the criticisms of for-profit colleges becoming irrelevant.

In addition, regulations for institutions receiving government support should also be fair in imposing the same rules across the board so as not to give some providers a competitive advantage over others. Adopting competition-friendly policies would permit consumers, rather than government administrators, to determine the success of a given institution and the allocation of scarce resources used for education.

There has been impropriety in profit-making colleges in the USA and opponents of such colleges in the UK have been keen to point this out. The result of this behaviour in the USA has been political interference, and in the UK there has been a slowing of reforms. The criticisms of the for-profit sector, however, lack any of the subtlety one would expect of sound academic analysis. While the ability of profit-making institutions to profit from government subsidies, while tolerating low completion rates, is one of the downsides of for-profit institutions, the critics ignore the huge benefits these institutions bring in opening up the higher education sector to minorities, the less well off and those whose family have had no engagement with the sector. Indeed, this opening up of the sector is, itself, bound to lead to lower completion rates. For-profit institutions are often treading where other institutions will not go. In addition, while the relative shortcomings of some aspects of for-profit institutions could be improved through better information provision, better results could also be obtained by changing the mechanism of providing government financing.

While we advocate that the UK should institute policies that make it more attractive for private investment to be made in higher education, the US experience suggests that such a policy needs to be crafted carefully to minimise instances of unethical and economic rent-seeking behaviour at the expense of taxpayers. All educational institutions receiving government subsidies should be held accountable for providing educational value. While defining educational value is a challenging task, it would be wise to incorporate results-oriented measures such as cost-effective success rates, academic achievement and post-graduation success. In addition, institutions should be required to publish this information so that prospective students, policymakers and employers can make better decisions on how to allocate scarce resources. But, as noted above, if we reduce government subsidies we automatically reduce the problems to which they can lead in the private and government sectors. Higher education subsidies that reward student failure and penalise success – like those the UK is introducing – may be especially unhelpful. The government subsidies encourage moral hazard on the part of the student, and this is not conducive to getting the best results out of either the for-profit or the non-profit sectors.

References

Bennett, D. L. (2009), 'Trends in the higher education labor force: identifying changes in worker composition and productivity', Washington, DC: The Center for College Affordability and Productivity, April.

Bennett, D. L., A. R. Lucchesi and R. K. Vedder (2010), 'For-profit higher education: growth innovation and regulation', Washington, DC: The Center for College Affordability and Productivity, July.

Brinner, R. (2010), 'Assessment of Missouri estimate of impact', Boston, MA: The Parthenon Group, 9 September.

Cellini, S. R., and C. Goldin (2012), 'Does federal student aid raise tuition? New evidence on for-profit colleges', NBER working paper 17827, February.

Guryan, J., and M. Thompson (2010), 'Report on gainful employment: executive summary', Charles River Associates, 29 March.

Kantrowitz, M. (2010), 'What is gainful employment? What is affordable debt?', student aid policy analysis, 1 March.

Kinser, K. (2006), *From Main Street to Wall Street: The Transformation of For-Profit Higher Education*, Hoboken: Wiley.

Lytle, R. (2010), 'Private sector post-secondary schools: do they deliver value to students and society?', Boston, MA: The Parthenon Group, March.

Mead, B., et al. (2009), *Evaluation of Evidence-Based Practices in Online Learning: A Meta-Analysis and Review of Online Learning Studies*, Washington, DC: US Department of Education, Office of Planning, Evaluation, and Policy Development.

Miller, B. (2010), 'Are you gainfully employed? Setting standards for for-profit degrees', Washington, DC: Education Sector, September.

Moore, R. W. (2005), 'The illusion of convergence: federal student aid policy in community colleges and proprietary schools', in *Community Colleges and Proprietary Schools: Conflict or Convergence?*, ed. D. A. Clowes and E. M. Hawthorne, San Francisco: Jossey-Bass, pp. 71–80.

Ruch, R. S. (2001), *Higher Ed, Inc.: The Rise of the For-Profit University*, Baltimore: Johns Hopkins University Press.

Turner, S. E. (2006), 'For-profit colleges in the contest of the market for higher education', in *Earnings from Learning: The Rise of For-Profit Universities*, ed. D. W. Breneman, B. Pusser and S. E. Turner, Albany: State University of New York Press.

Twigg, C. A. (2005), 'Course redesign improves learning and reduces cost', The National Center for Public Policy and Higher Education, June.

Watson, S. S. (2009), 'Graduating at-risk students: a cross-sector analysis', Washington, DC: Imagine America Foundation.

PART 3: NEW MODELS OF EDUCATION

8 WHY IS THERE NO IKEA IN EDUCATION?

Anders Hultin

When Ingvar Kamprad founded IKEA in 1943, no one expected that his idea to deliver self-assembly flat-pack furniture to customers would have an impact on millions of households all over the world. Fifty years on, however, IKEA is not only opening new warehouses but now has 127,000 employees and annual revenues of €23.5 billion, and has transformed a global industry by making cheap, functional and designed furniture available to people who previously could not afford it. So why do we not have similar success stories to IKEA in the world of education?

Three key approaches

There are three key approaches or incentive systems that are applied to school operations within the state-funded tier of the education system: a state model driven by political incentives based on extensive state involvement in the delivery of education; a semi-private approach driven by philanthropic incentives where schools tend to be owned and operated by charitable trusts in symbiosis with the state; and a market model driven by profit incentives based on competition, choice and private investments.

The motivation behind the state model is to make sure that good education is provided for all regardless of wealth and background. State involvement is believed to be a guarantee that all schools can provide a minimum standard. The state seeks to achieve this by introducing floor standards and striving to develop programmes that foster the development of equality in terms of provision. This is, for example, why state systems tend to distribute more resources where circumstances are more challenging.

There are two key things that are not normally encouraged under the state model – competition and choice. Why should schools compete? Head teachers and teachers are supposed to collaborate – not compete – and work together for the common purpose of preparing young people for their future under the framework of a national curriculum. As for choice – parental choice undermines the whole idea behind the state model as it indirectly confirms that high-quality education is not equally distributed across all schools.

Unfortunately, high-quality education is not distributed equally. Good schools get a good reputation and become over-subscribed. As a result they become more selective about whom they admit, or the house prices in their catchment area increase to a level that only certain people can afford – these schools are in a positive spiral and become occupied, on the whole, by more affluent families. Bad schools operating under a 'per pupil funding regime' become desperate to fill their places to survive, so they end up offering places to pupils that have no alternatives or those that have been refused by good schools. They fall into a negative spiral. Often it is the poorer families who are left having to send their children to these schools.

The power of these spirals is evident in the day-to-day life of many head teachers. These spirals are exacerbated for two reasons. One is that the supply side is fairly static – the inflow and outflow of new provision is very limited, so schools in positive spirals are rarely challenged and those struggling with a negative trend tend to be hand-held through all kinds of interventions and support initiatives. The other reason is because people tend to watch and replicate what other people are doing in order to deal with risk and to make life a bit easier. Parents become suspicious about schools that are not full and impressed by schools with long waiting lists. To compensate for lack of knowledge and information they trust the behaviour of others and act as part of a pack.

The problem is that the state model works like a static, zero-sum game. The role of the authorities is to match supply and demand. Their natural instinct is to establish the perfect balance between the two. Overcapacity within the state model is a failure of planning and is regarded as a waste of money. The introduction of the need to account for parental choice is therefore not only a distraction but also a lottery that produces winners and losers. Extensive opportunities for parents to choose a school for their children within this environment will most likely further stratify the system and cause a threat to the idea, and the value, behind the state model.

Despite the achievements of a pure state model in countries such as Finland (which is the top performer in the Programme for International Student Assessment, often known as PISA), some have come to question this approach to education. State monopolies are not seen to be the only way to organise the delivery of 21st-century education, with diversity and pluralism increasingly required to meet the demands of an ever more complex society and future. This is probably why many education systems over the last few decades have changed their basic rules and regulations.

They have started to look to the private sector and, step by step, have introduced more and more characteristics of a market model.

Deregulation and the philanthropic model

Even though the funding system in many countries is still based on taxation, many school systems are going through a process of deregulation, and more power and autonomy are being given to schools. As a consequence the state is redefining its role – from that of an operator to more that of a facilitator – and this transition means that we are now somewhere between the old-fashioned state model and an untested market model. This compromise is what I call the philanthropic model.

An illustrative example of this approach to state education was the introduction of the Academy programme in England in 2003. Broadly speaking, a failing state school was simply closed and replaced by a new school, typically in an expensive, new building. In parallel, a new legal entity was created, often a charitable trust, and a sponsor was appointed to control the trust. The motivation behind this movement was to drive improvement in the weakest schools by providing individuals, companies or organisations with the opportunity to 'give back' to society. In the first phase of this programme these sponsors were supposed to make a financial contribution of £2 million and provide their 'expertise' free of charge to the school. Under this initiative individuals from sectors such as the car and carpet industries became school operators. It was assumed that their success in the 'private sector' would benefit schools and that their desire to 'give back' to society would act as a driver for their long-term involvement.

Since its formation in May 2010 the coalition government has listed new requirements of individuals or groups if they want to sponsor an Academy. Importantly, these include new sponsors being able to demonstrate a proven track-record in education. While this has made it more complicated for philanthropists to become involved in education, it has also opened up the appeal of Academy sponsorship to a new sector and has resulted in universities and high-performing schools showing an interest in sponsorship. The growth in the number of schools qualifying for Academy status means that increasing numbers of schools are no longer controlled by their local authorities and a new level of diversity in provision is being introduced.

A second new programme that has been introduced is the 'free schools' programme. Under this initiative parent groups can build a case for setting up a school, provide evidence and then apply to the Department for Education for funding. The growth in numbers created under this initiative has been much slower than some anticipated, but the first free schools were opened in September 2011. This development represents a fundamental shift in the English school system. We are witnessing a significant migration of schools from state control to independence and from state ownership to some kind of private ownership. For those responsible the purpose of this migration is to capture the 'good' side of the market, i.e. introducing choice and diversity, while protecting schools and pupils from what politicians seem to think of as the 'bad': the profit motive.

Can we be sure, however, that this state of affairs will actually bring the benefits of a market system, but avoid the perceived downsides? Or is there a risk, when a home-cooked mix of state involvement, philanthropy and market-inspired ideas is introduced, that this model will not have the benefits of either the state or the market model?

Great schools and how to make them

Although some people find it hard to agree about what exactly a great school is, and many parents find that the league tables promoted by governments are not a sufficient way of describing what really makes a good school, the concept of a great school is relatively well entrenched in national and international mindsets. And there are thousands and thousands of great schools in the world. The problem is, we just haven't worked out a way to replicate the great schools that we have. As I know the Swedish school market well, I want to illustrate this point by telling the story of Carlsson School in Stockholm.

Carlsson School in Stockholm was established more than a hundred years ago. It was one of the few private schools that survived the nationalisation wave that hit private schools in Sweden in the 1960s and 1970s. When the free school reform was introduced in 1992, Carlsson School converted to the scheme and became state-funded. The school is very popular and is always at the top of the national league tables. Since the voucher system requires a school to adopt very strict admission principles, Carlsson School has introduced a waiting list for parents. The list, based on a principle of first come, first served, is strictly applied by the school.

The waiting list indicates that Carlsson School might be one of these great schools. The challenge we are faced with is that these great schools tend not to expand as a means of making their success available to more pupils. Instead they enjoy their positive spiral and the comfort of their waiting list and then focus on other things. Why would they risk their success with new adventures and challenges elsewhere? The Carlsson schools have no motive for growth. For them growth represents a risk, not an opportunity. Furthermore, their success and 'know-how' are locked into a charitable trust, controlled by their trustees, guided by charitable constitutions formulated more than a hundred years ago.

One key question in this context is: are great schools replicable or is their success mainly a reflection of great leaders and hence difficult or impossible to replicate? This question is highly relevant in the current political context. The direction of British government policy is to abolish top-down management of schools by the state and instead promote 'cross-fertilisation' as a way to improve schools on a larger scale. The success of this strategy will be dependent on whether or not these schools are able to understand the key drivers of their success; describe and decode these methodologies; package them; and make them accessible to colleagues in other schools.

Thankfully, we are now beginning to see the emergence of some recipes for successful school operations. The ARK Group of Academies might be one. They claim that they have developed a recipe for turning around failing schools in poor suburbs of London. If such a recipe exists there are millions of children living in poor circumstances in the suburbs of big cities around the world who are suffering from poor education and in desperate need of turnaround schools and recipes for success. The difficulty is that ARK, a charitable trust, at least in the short term is not expecting to expand beyond fifteen secondary schools. Fifteen schools, in a school system with over three thousand secondary schools, will not have a systemic impact.

Not all Academy groups are as modest as ARK. Some of them are aiming for real scale and talking about having hundreds of schools under their umbrella. But why is that? It is sometimes difficult to understand why these groups, often led by successful and well-paid head teachers, are so keen to become big. For an outsider it is often difficult to understand the real purpose and incentives of a charitable trust. We know that companies are for-profit and we therefore understand the purpose of these entities. We know that state operations are led by politicians and politicians are accountable to voters and taxpayers, so we can broadly understand the motivations and incentives behind a state school. But things are far less clear with a charitable trust.

What we do know is that the growth of these Academy groups is not driven by a demand expressed by parents and pupils. Their growth is mainly driven by the Department for Education. The secretary of state has found reasons and evidence to transfer schools from the state domain to these charitable trusts and head teachers. There are no reasons to question whether these trusts are carefully chosen by the secretary of state. But there are good reasons to ask whether this transition will work in the long term. What will happen when the founders of and the key people behind successful Academy groups have left or when the sponsor of a school is not interested any more, or lacks the capacity to play the role of a sponsor?

The challenge on a macro level must be to invent a mechanism that makes sure that excellence achieved in one school can be transferred to another, that success is replicated and scaled so that as many schools as possible can benefit from the achievements of others and avoid repeating mistakes and reinventing the wheel. It should be possible to work out a formula for achieving real and sustainable improvement on a systemic level, but the complexity of this task should not be underestimated. Transforming our school system in this way will also require skills and a new cohort of leaders different from those normally represented in education.

Assuming that these recipes or formulae for great schools actually exist, do we have an evolutionary system that will make sure that these recipes will spread and flourish while others that are found to be less successful disappear?

Arguments against a market model

The major argument against a market model being introduced in the school system is the perceived conflict between the shareholders' interests and the interests of the pupils. Since the profit motive in education rarely has any advocates this argument has not really been challenged and investigated. The lack of any real discussion has left the field open for very simple, populist arguments to flourish. Central to these is the argument that making a profit and paying dividends to shareholders represent a lost opportunity to improve a child's education. The assumption made is that there is a strong correlation between quality of education and spending and that money spent is a key driver of success.

Research undertaken, for example by the OECD/PISA, indicates that the correlation between money spent and quality is weak and not very obvious. Indeed, their work shows that there are many other factors that are more important for outcomes than the amount of money spent. Numerous studies show that the size of a class does not really have a big impact on outcomes (only when class sizes come down to a level of twelve to thirteen do they start to have an impact on outcomes), or at least that there are many other factors that have a stronger impact on how much pupils learn – the quality of the teachers; the leadership in a school; the amount of support provided to pupils and teachers, etc. This is good news. Even limited amounts of money can provide high-quality education under the right circumstances.

As the CEO of Kunskapsskolan, the school chain described by Mr Peje Emilsson in another chapter of this book, I had the unique opportunity to investigate correlations between spending and school performance. This was because the Kunskapsskolan model is a chain model that is replicated across all schools no matter how big the voucher (per pupil fund) from each local municipality. The spread of the voucher amount was huge, so one could really compare like for like. During this period I found that the most profitable school was one with only an average per pupil fund from the local municipality. The same school, however, had the best academic results and among the most satisfied pupils, parents and teachers. Their success was not only relative to other schools in the group – pupil grades defined the school as one of the top 30 schools in Sweden.

This was simply a great school, and since the school was good in all aspects they did not waste money. There was no slack in the system. Instead there was a tight team of teachers working together with a shared mission. The school made sure that they had the pupils they needed and that they kept and maintained their good reputation among future parents, so they always had enough applications for the next year.

The profit motive and academic results

Across the group of 27 schools, we could see a similar pattern between profit and academic results, as well as between weak profits (sometimes losses) and poor academic results. Good schools were profitable and they contrasted with some of the lower-performing schools that did not attract as many families (of course) and provided weaker financial returns for shareholders (it is worth noting that most comparisons of schools within the group were on a relative basis and that local circumstances never provided an excuse for bad performance). The absolute performance of the group is strong: 90 per cent of its schools are among the top three in their municipalities and 50 per cent of the schools are among the top 100 in the country.

At the heart of the Kunskapsskolan model is the pupil log book. This book serves as a centrepiece for every pupil's plans and learning strategies. I remember at one point one of my colleagues concluded all ongoing discussions in the management team about quality correlations by saying 'ignore the cash book, focus on the log book'. This short phrase also summarises my argument. In a competitive environment profit reflects quality – never the other way around. Armed with this experience I find it hard to believe that there is an in-built conflict between the profit motive and quality. In reality it is the other way around; without the motivation of profit the quality of delivery can be jeopardised.

The profit motive has served us well in other parts of society, driving many of the most advanced, complicated and highly regarded developments and technologies. So why does it remain the case that it is fine to make profits from a construction company building schools, but not from a company investing in one of the most important assets of all – the education that goes on in these buildings? Why is it that we accept and even admire people who are successful and get rich from all kinds of industries and sectors, but that we make a moral judgement against people doing the same from something that is important and for the common good: the future of our children?

Courage of convictions or compromise?

When faced with the choice between the state and market models politicians need to have the courage of their convictions. If the agenda is to provide choice and a variety of alternatives for parents, diversity in terms of provision and competition among schools, it is worthwhile recognising that these aspects are part of a wider, more complex and highly sophisticated ecosystem that is not easy for politicians to design and impose. The market model will provide the incentive system that ensures continual and systemic improvement, but will also bring new challenges as well as a requirement for the state to redefine its role and responsibilities.

If the agenda is to provide a compromise between the two models there are clear risks involved. More choice without more schools could have the opposite of the intended impact, creating further stratification and widening the gap between poor and rich people as well as lowering the total performance of the system. To introduce competition when the basics of the system require collaboration between neighbouring schools could be counter-productive and may conserve the high level of fragmentation in the school system. But, most importantly, success achieved within charitable trusts funded by taxpayers but beyond their control may make it even harder to ensure that these examples of progress and excellence are translated into system-wide improvements.

Returning to my initial question, why do we not have any IKEAs in the world of education? The simple answer is that real entrepreneurs are locked out of this key sector since their incentives and motivations are regarded as a threat to both schools and pupils. I wonder what the expansion of IKEA would have looked like, however, if it had been set up as a charitable trust with the purpose of helping people to get cheap furniture – and I wonder what this furniture would look like today.

9 UK BUSINESS SCHOOLS NEED AN INJECTION OF THE PROFIT MOTIVE

J. R. Shackleton

Introduction

UK business schools can appear to be a success story. More than one hundred such schools teach around 15 per cent of all the students in higher education. They account for a large proportion of the international students studying in the UK, and through partnerships and franchises in dozens of countries worldwide they make a further contribution to the UK's balance of trade (Williams, 2010). They have grown rapidly over the last 25 years, and demand for their undergraduate and postgraduate programmes remains buoyant.

In addition to degree programmes, these schools provide substantial amounts of professional and executive education, training and short courses, and are engaged in consultancy worldwide. Many are engaged in business incubation and start-ups and make a range of other contributions to regional and local economic development (Cooke and Galt, 2010). They generate large amounts of highly rated research: British business schools do well in international rankings.

But all is not quite as rosy as it seems. I shall argue in this chapter that our university-based business schools are often too detached from business, over-academic and unnecessarily expensive. They do not give students or employers as good a service as they might expect, have not innovated sufficiently rapidly in a changing market, and their considerable earning power is often used inappropriately to cross-subsidise other university subjects.

Here, I put the case for moving schools out of the university sector and injecting the profit motive into their activities, and suggest ways in which this might be done.

What is wrong?

Our business schools are, in reality, far from perfect. Employers complain that their graduates are not properly prepared for work, and many struggle to find good employment. According to the Higher Education Statistics Agency, the unemployment rate for 2009/10 business graduates six months after graduation is, at 10.5 per cent, above the average of 9.1 per cent for all graduates. Entry standards are not particularly high, and the quality of academic work produced sometimes leaves something to be desired. Students complain that much of their study is irrelevant and that they are taught by people who have little experience of business, certainly at a high level. Although there is much good practice to be cited, student evaluations in the National Student Satisfaction Survey suggest that business teaching, at the undergraduate level in particular, is not always very inspiring. There is also relatively little of it (12.3 hours per week against an all-subject average of 14.2 hours in 2007) and it takes place disproportionately in large groups. Nor do students compensate by working hard in private: the total amount of hours spent in study is the second-lowest of any subject group.

Staff are increasingly recruited on the basis of their academic qualifications and their aptitude for research of a kind which gets published in high-ranking journals or attracts research council funding, but which may have little relevance to business or to teaching. Links with companies are in some cases fitful and limited. Business people certainly have little or no influence in the running of business schools, and they spend much more of their training or consultancy budgets on commercial providers than on business schools, which are often slow and inflexible in response to rapidly changing demand.

At the undergraduate level, work placements, though widely recognised as one of the best ways of preparing students for employment, have declined in popularity as students facing high fees seek shorter courses and the opportunity to work part-time in bars and retail stores. University business schools have been slow to adjust to this reality and to innovate to support new student lifestyles.

At postgraduate level, classes are often dominated by overseas students while UK students are either uninterested in the courses on offer or unable to afford the high fees charged. In no programme is this more apparent than in the erstwhile business school flagship, the Master of Business Administration (MBA). This was introduced from the USA with the intention of revitalising and upskilling experienced British management. The highest-rated MBA in the country, the full-time award offered by the London Business School, enrolled just 9 per cent of its 2010/11 intake from the UK. Most other schools could paint a similar picture, except that the academic background of their entrants and the quality of their previous business experience would probably be a good deal weaker.

Many of these problems arise from the institutional location of business schools. With a limited number of exceptions, most

UK schools are integrated firmly into the university sector. This has a number of benefits – it means that overhead costs are shared, that qualifications have widespread credibility, and that staff are integrated into a broader academic community with traditions of scholarship, open-mindedness and ethical behaviour – but it has a considerable downside. Although for government accounting purposes, which extend beyond the UK to the OECD's classification, universities are counted in the private sector, in many ways our universities behave rather too much like public sector organisations.

This means that they have become over-dependent on government funding, and continually concerned about 'cuts'. Many staff remain resistant to notions of consumer sovereignty. They have generous pensions and other conditions of service, with incremental pay scales which allow little scope for reward for outstanding performance. Conversely, poor performance is too often tolerated. This is in part because academic staff are heavily unionised, and collectively negotiated procedures for managing poor performance are unwieldy and ineffective – much to the annoyance of more highly committed staff. Academics expect to pick and choose a limited number of teaching engagements, set well in advance and only between October and May: unions often insist on overtime payments for teaching 'outside the national contract' – i.e. at weekends or in the summer.

As quasi-government bodies, university schools are also subject to a range of government directives over matters such as widening participation, the Public Sector Equality Duty, procurement obligations, environmental sustainability, and so forth: this raises costs and can detract from focus on core business.

Finally, within universities, business schools have little

independence and are subject to a variety of irksome institutional policies in relation to important practical matters such as estates, marketing, recruitment and human resource management, information technology, finance and student accommodation, as well as academic issues such as departmental structure, the provision of modular degrees and credit structures and the length of the academic year.

Deans have limited authority and are subject to pressures from powerful vice-chancellors above and from independently minded and outspoken staff and demanding students below. Most do not have the power to set student fees and have little control over budgets, which are usually determined at university level and offer little scope for retaining any extra funds brought in, or for offering higher-quality facilities to business clients.

It is widely believed (Matthews, 2011) to be common practice for business schools to be treated as 'cash cows' by the rest of the university, with their surpluses subsidising other faculties and schools which for historical reasons (or because of the government higher education funding body's bands) often have more generous staffing ratios and/or better accommodation. Apart from the problems this creates for business schools, it is arguably sharp practice, given that overseas postgraduate students, for example, are frequently paying very high fees which they could reasonably expect to see reflected in the resources allocated to their teaching and facilities.

Perhaps more fundamentally, there is surely something of a paradox in the fact that mainstream business education in this country – largely aimed at preparing young people (and young people who display a strong commitment to business, with many of them wishing eventually to start their own companies) for work in a market economy – should be in the hands of institutions which do not fully engage with that economy and for which there is no profit objective to focus and discipline their collective efforts. I argue that this has restricted choice for individuals, and has raised the costs of studying when technological and organisational developments in the wider economy should have lowered them. It benefits 'producers' at a cost to 'consumers' – whether the latter be students, their families or future employers.

The early development of university-based business schools

How did we get to this position? Commercial subjects have been taught at a high level in British colleges and universities for a long time, well back into the nineteenth century. These subjects were taught in a variety of contexts: in university faculties of humanities, engineering or economics; in commercial colleges in both the government and private sector; and in the early polytechnics of the first decade of the twentieth century. The modern concept of the business school is, however, a post-war development in this country. As such, it is a development of its time in two respects: firstly, it is a deliberate government intervention because of a belief in market failure; and, secondly, it is an uncritical import from the USA.

The early 1960s was a period when politicians of both parties supported new forms of government intervention in the economy in response to the relatively poor performance of the UK compared with other economies. One feature of this was the establishment of the tripartite – big business, big union and big government representation – National Economic Development Council

(NEDC). In April 1963 the NEDC, diagnosing poor management as one of the country's failings and arguing that inadequate training and education were part of the problem, proposed the establishment of a high-level business school in imitation of US models such as Harvard Business School. In the same year the Robbins Committee recommended that two postgraduate schools be set up. There was some difference of opinion over the form of institution proposed. Many industrialists did not want to see the schools as part of the university sector, but more as free-standing outfits similar to the Administrative Staff College, which had been founded at Henley in the 1940s. They were prepared to put up their own money to do this.

The Franks Report, however, hurriedly produced to adjudicate on this issue, came down in favour of establishing two postgraduate schools (in London and in Manchester) as part of existing universities, albeit with a considerable degree of autonomy. The London Business School subsequently developed much greater freedom than its Manchester counterpart, breaking away from the University of London and getting its own Royal Charter in 1986. Despite providing generous initial financial support (worth the equivalent of over £60 million in today's money), business exerted little influence on the subsequent development of the two schools, which consciously modelled their offerings – in particular the MBA – on those of the top US university-based schools. Other possible models, such as the regionally based French business schools, umbilically linked to chambers of commerce and operating outside the university system, were not on the agenda.

The twenty years following the designation of the London and Manchester schools saw several developments. The numbers of students in these two schools grew only very slowly, and by the mid-1980s were well below the levels which Franks had projected for them. On the other hand, more than twenty other business or management schools were now teaching postgraduates in the university sector, including Warwick, City University (later Cass Business School), Aston and other new universities and former Colleges of Advanced Technology. Moreover, in the 1970s there had been a rapid expansion of undergraduate business studies degrees, particularly in the polytechnic sector, where the Council for National Academic Awards (CNAA) validated many of these programmes. As yet, however, undergraduate business, accounting and economics degrees were often taught by different staff from those teaching older postgraduate and post-experience business and management students (on programmes such as the Diploma in Management Studies or professional qualifications). These undergraduate teachers were usually located elsewhere in the university, in schools or faculties of social science or commerce.

Despite these positive developments, criticism of business schools grew in the mid-1980s as it became apparent that they had not made a fundamental impact on management training or visibly improved the quality of business decision-making. The MBA had not really caught on with employers, and it was felt that many teaching staff were out of touch, jargon-ridden and too interested in esoteric research. The academic system of tenure exacerbated this. Protected by state funding, university-based schools were perceived as insensitive to the needs of business and their students. They acted as an implicit cartel and did not compete over fees, institutionalising inefficiency and raising costs. It was felt by some that a fundamental error had been made by Franks in locating schools in the university sector.

It was against this background that the Institute of Economic Affairs published a Hobart Paper by two business academics, Brian (later Lord) Griffiths and Hugh Murray, from City University. They made a case for privatising postgraduate business education, creating discrete schools with the status of independent legal entities outside the government sector and, after a three-year withdrawal period, receiving no current government funding for teaching – although Griffiths and Murray argued for a capital endowment to set the schools on their way. They also argued that research was a public good and that the new schools should be eligible for grants from the then Economic and Social Research Council (Griffiths and Murray, 1985).

Salaries and conditions of employment should be determined by the schools themselves, outside university negotiations. In particular, they argued for a wider range of types of contract and an end to semi-automatic tenure.

The Griffiths/Murray proposals were a significant break in the statist consensus surrounding business schools, and indeed the university sector more generally. They attracted a good deal of attention, notably from Sir Keith Joseph, at the time the Secretary of State for Education and Science and an early advocate of many of the changes in higher education which have become commonplace today. Despite this high-level support, however, the privatisation proposals were sidelined. On reflection, although they were a useful step forward, it can be argued that they were weak in three ways.

Firstly, Griffiths and Murray were interested only in postgraduate business education, leaving the numerically much larger area of undergraduate studies to the old university sector. But the arguments for linking business education closely to business practice are as strong – possibly stronger – at the undergraduate level than at the postgraduate level. When Griffiths and Murray wrote, most postgraduate students would have had some significant work experience, but it was possible (and indeed still is) in many UK business schools for undergraduate and some postgraduate students to go through their degrees without any significant contact with business people. This surely cannot be an adequate preparation for careers.

Secondly, the proposers still saw a need for some state support, through capital and research funding. But experience suggests that such funding always comes with a cat's cradle of strings attached. In particular it seems unlikely that large capital endowments would be made available without close supervision of the uses to which these funds would be put.

Thirdly, the form which the privatised schools would take was left vague: only one paragraph was devoted to it. The favoured suggestion (ibid.: 53) seems to have been for schools 'to seek charity status and become companies limited by guarantee on the lines of the London Business School', although 'private companies, or partnerships of staff' were mentioned as possibilities. What is clear, however, is that private for-profit schools were not as yet envisaged as the model. Privatisation was seen as a means of cutting the need for state funding, for making postgraduate students and employers pay more, and for freeing schools from university structures. But the proposed independent business schools were not seen as profit-making entities in their own right.

Developments since the 1980s

Since Griffiths and Murray were writing, UK business schools have changed almost beyond recognition. For one thing, the scale is very different. The numbers undertaking undergraduate and postgraduate study in business subjects have risen more than threefold, while the number of schools has also risen sharply, with well over one hundred schools now members of the Association of Business Schools (Williams, 2010). A large part of this expansion has come from the post-1992 sector. Most of the rapidly growing ex-polytechnics and newer colleges chose in the 1990s to consolidate their undergraduate and postgraduate business and management teaching in the form of an all-through business school. The mid-1980s Manchester Business School had fewer than three hundred students, all postgraduate, and forty-odd staff. One of the larger new university business schools may have 3,000–4,000 undergraduates and another 1,000–1,500 postgraduates on campus, with many more distance-learning or franchised students. It will employ well over two hundred academic staff.

These staff are different from those appointed in the past. The tendency towards an emphasis on academic rather than practical learning was apparent by the mid-1980s, but it has strengthened considerably as a result of generational change. New entrants are now increasingly drawn from an academic, rather than a business, background. A doctorate and a number of research publications are seen by many, perhaps most, university business schools as an entry-level requirement. This is driven in large part by the Research Assessment Exercise (now renamed the Research Excellence Framework), which awards government funding based on the quality of research, as assessed by panels of peer reviewers who place emphasis on originality of technique (particularly quantitative technique) above practical relevance. The amounts of money obtained by most business schools as a result of research evaluation are trivial in most cases, but all universities feel that they must devote disproportionate resources in an endeavour to gain the highest possible ranking. This may be more for academics' prestige than for its educational results: a regular complaint, particularly at the most research-intensive schools, is that students are taught by postgraduates and junior staff, never seeing the research stars of whom the institution boasts.

Another dramatic change is the internationalisation of business schools, part of a wider globalisation of higher education. The UK has done well from this, with Britain being second only to the USA as a student destination, and its business schools have become major players internationally. International rankings of schools are watched carefully, and most of the top schools are accredited with overseas bodies such as the USA's Association to Advance Collegiate Schools of Business (AACSB) and the European Foundation for Management Development (EFMD). Staff are increasingly drawn from abroad as well, attracted in part by the opportunity for research, which is downplayed in many overseas institutions.

This internationalisation means that the original focus of UK business schools – the improvement of elite British management, as advocated by the NEDC and the Franks Report – has shifted. The need is rather to educate a very diverse range of students, British and international, for a jobs market which is constantly changing and is worldwide rather than local. Most of today's business schools operate abroad as well as within the UK – either running programmes and courses directly in overseas locations, or franchising degrees to partner colleges throughout the world. It is a market which places increasing emphasis on qualifications, yet also on individual enterprise, rather than preparation for a defined set of occupations and roles.

A further significant change, related to the growing number of international students, is the reduced dependency of business schools on direct government funding through the Higher Education Funding Council for England (HEFCE) and equivalent bodies in the other parts of the UK. Even before the current round of spending cuts, which will reduce virtually to zero the direct support that business subjects receive in England, most business schools – unlike other parts of their parent universities – received the bulk of their income from student fees, franchises, government and private research funding, payments for training, consultancy, conferences and short courses. In this sense they are much better equipped than most other parts of universities to face the new higher education funding environment – and also better positioned for privatisation than at the time Griffiths and Murray were writing.

Yet another – and, in the context of this discussion, very significant – change since the 1980s has been the gradual incursion into higher education of private providers. Worldwide, it has been estimated that around 30 per cent of total global enrolment in higher education is now in the private (non-state) sector (Universities UK, 2010: 61). This has been most marked in, though by no means exclusive to, business education. The majority of this provision is by not-for-profit institutions, but the fastest-growing part of the market in the USA in recent years, for example, has been for-profit – which now accounts for around 20 per cent of all private US higher education (Taylor, 2009).

Private providers in the UK

Private business schools are prestigious institutions in France, where HEC Paris and INSEAD dominate the rankings, and to a lesser extent in Spain and Germany. In the UK they remain something of a novelty, although some of them have been operating for many years.

The independent University of Buckingham has a small business school which is one of only a handful of non-government sector members of the UK's Association of Business Schools. Buckingham has been a private, not-for-profit provider with a Royal Charter since 1983, and is the 'public face' of private higher education in this country. This is rather misleading in some ways. Buckingham has demonstrated very clearly, by successfully (and voluntarily) facing Quality Assurance Agency audit, and by topping the National Student Satisfaction Survey, that its standards are equivalent to, or higher than, most government sector higher education providers. It has also made some attractive innovations in the delivery of higher education, most notably the two-year degree and the ability to teach four-term years while still enabling staff to conduct research. The institution is not typical of private providers, however: it remains tiny, with fewer than a thousand students in total, and has not had a great deal of influence on the rest of the sector.

Buckingham is a 'not-for-profit' with limited ambitions for expansion. Another small-scale non-profit provider is Ashridge Business School, which awards its own postgraduate degrees and has a deserved reputation with top FTSE companies, for whom it provides executive education and consultancy. There are other not-for-profit providers which occupy a different market position, such as the European Business School London (EBS), which is part of the Regent's College group, which do not award their own degrees but teach programmes validated by other institutions – in

EBS's case by the Open University. There are also a number of overseas universities offering business degrees within the UK.

There are at least thirty other private business schools in the UK, many of which are for-profits which specialise in providing places for international students on UK-validated franchise programmes at considerably lower cost than similar on-campus programmes at the universities that validate them. They are able to do this because they are usually lean operations, using less expensive premises more intensively than UK university business schools, having several entry points throughout the year, and teaching at weekends. Their staff, though reasonably well paid, have individual contracts and teach throughout the year. They make considerable use of part-time staff. The best of these schools make good use of information technology and offer strong student support, while minimising the growth of management layers and in-house functions (human resources, marketing and so on) which have led many university schools to be top-heavy.

There is one for-profit business school which can award its own degrees. This is BPP, which has long had a formidable reputation for the quality of its preparation for professional business (and law) examinations. It now has university college status. BPP, which was publicly quoted in the UK but has now been acquired by the US-owned Apollo Group, has four campuses around the UK and has pioneered very flexible undergraduate and postgraduate degrees which enable students to progress at their own pace and combine both face-to-face small-group teaching and e-learning. It has a strong core of permanent staff, who can engage in research, but again makes use of business professionals as part-timers. It offers degrees at the same price as current UK/EU fee levels, but does not receive any direct government funding through HEFCE.

Table 1 **Types of UK business school, 2011**

Classification	*Example*
• University-based, degree-awarding, undergraduate and postgraduate, not-for-profit	Pre-1992: Aston Business School Post-1992: Nottingham Business School (Nottingham Trent University) Distance learning: Open University Business School Private: University of Buckingham Business School Also: In-house awards for companies; programmes franchised to public sector FE colleges.
• Free-standing, postgraduate only, not-for-profit	Ashridge Business School
• Overseas universities offering degrees in UK, not-for-profit	Chicago Booth School of Business
• Undergraduate and postgraduate, for-profit, franchised degrees	London School of Business and Finance
• Undergraduate and postgraduate, degree-awarding, for-profit	BPP Business School

It already recruits many UK students, unlike most other for-profit providers, and the implication is that it will be in a very strong position to undercut university business schools as higher fees come in.

Table 1 summarises the range of providers currently operating in the UK. At the moment probably 10–15 per cent of all business students are in private schools. In addition to teaching students, however, there are other ways in which private businesses are involved in higher education provision. For example, there are various private sector companies which support distance-learning platforms for university business schools, which run pre-entry

English and study skills courses for their overseas students, or which help recruit students (especially in overseas markets, where local agents are widely employed).

There has been a noticeable change in attitude towards private and, more particularly, for-profit higher education provision in recent years. It was the last Labour government which took the initial political risk of introducing top-up fees, and it also took the first tentative step in favour of boosting the private sector when it gave BPP degree-awarding powers in 2007. Towards the end of its period in government, its *Higher Ambitions* document noted that:

> Alongside the development of our publicly funded universities and colleges we also see an important role for fully private providers over the next 10–15 years. The Government has made it possible for such providers to obtain degree awarding powers. We see no reason why this type of provision should not grow in the future and provide greater choice for students and employers, adding to innovation and diversity in the range of HE options available.[1]

More surprisingly, perhaps, in March 2010 Universities UK, the lobby group for the sector, issued a report on private and for-profit higher education provision which offered a broadly favourable view of existing activities and set out various scenarios for the future expansion of private provision, including the acquisition of publicly funded institutions by private providers. It concluded with 22 recommendations for representative groups, publicly funded institutions, accreditation bodies, government and private providers (Universities UK, 2010). The Higher Education Policy

1 Department for Business Innovation and Skills (2009), p. 104.

Institute has also recently produced a report (Middlehurst and Fielden, 2011) arguing for a new regulatory framework for private provision, recognising the legitimate role of for-profit providers.

And the coalition government has made it clear that it sees a stronger role for private providers. David Willetts has said:

> It is healthy to have a vibrant private sector working alongside our more traditional universities. International experience shows a diverse range of higher education providers helps widen access, focuses attention on teaching quality and promotes innovative learning methods.[2]

Mr Willetts has also suggested that private companies should be given contracts to take over failing government sector universities or colleges and restore them to financial stability.

The way forward

Against this exciting background, what conclusions can we draw for the future of UK business schools?

Continuing government involvement in higher education might be rationalised by belief that the market fails in one or more of three ways. First, there could be quality issues because of asymmetric information; secondly, there may be significant externalities; and thirdly, there may be capital market failings which prevent poorer potential students entering university as they cannot raise sufficient capital to cover the costs because they lack collateral for a loan. Are these strong enough reasons to keep business schools in the quasi-government university sector?

2 *Times Higher Education* (2010).

The first argument is far less plausible than it may have been in the past, as a result of the spread of information through the Web. It is also clear that, in business education at least, the sector is well capable of generating accreditation mechanisms without the need for the government-sponsored bodies such as the QAA. We have already noted school-wide international accreditation systems such as that of AACSB and EFMD, but business education also has impressive systems for specific qualifications, such as those operated by the Association of MBAs, the Chartered Institute of Personnel and Development and the various professional accounting bodies.

Are there externalities? There are sometimes claims made for external cultural benefits being generated by arts and humanities subjects, but in business the main argument seems to have been that good-quality management education can boost economic growth. While there may conceivably be some grain of truth in this, it does not follow that this education should be provided by institutions which are funded and controlled by the state. The huge demand for business education, spilling over into the private sector, does not indicate that it needs to be artificially stimulated by government in the way that, say, the science, technology, engineering and mathematics subjects are subsidised.

The issue about student funding is an important one, and there may indeed be a case for the government ensuring that all those qualified to enter higher education should have access to loans. This does not, however, mean that such loans should necessarily be subsidised significantly by the taxpayer – especially in this field. Business and management students are more committed to higher-earning careers than many other groups of students: they typically do not study because of academic interest in their subject in the same way as, say, arts students. There is already some private sector support for career loans for postgraduate business and management students, and, in principle, it ought to be possible to extend this much more widely.

There is also a very strong argument for saying that some of the risk of students failing programmes, defaulting on loans or being unable to repay loans should be borne by the institution that admits the student (see Shephard, 2010). This might act to raise standards in schools and also might prevent some of the scams which have occurred with student loans systems in private for-profit schools in the USA (see Middlehurst and Fielden, 2011). It would mean that government backing for loans to business students could be greatly reduced, if not abolished completely.

Theoretical arguments about market failure do not, therefore, constitute a case for keeping business schools within the publicly controlled university sector. The arguments which Griffiths and Murray made for privatisation over a quarter of a century ago have been strengthened by the way in which university-based business schools have developed as high-cost operations with insufficient links with business, excessive emphasis on esoteric research and inadequate customer care. Yet they are also paradoxically better prepared for privatisation than their predecessors as government funding has been restricted, the world market for higher education has opened up, and schools have been forced to explore new sources of funding.

I would argue that the best form for this privatisation to take is the profit-maximising enterprise, the institutional shape which has proved most successful historically across a wide range of goods and services provision. What this can bring to business education is a stronger customer focus, cost control, expertise from other service areas, links with other businesses and new sources of capital. Other independent formats are clearly possible, and even perhaps desirable as a first step towards a freer market in business education. But not-for-profits tend to concentrate on niches (for example, Ashridge and Buckingham) rather than focus on the mass market which is today's business education sector. Not-for-profits also suffer from a shortage of new capital.

Private alumni donations are an important source of capital in the USA, but in the UK such donations have been 'crowded out' by the expectation of government provision and an unfavourable tax regime. As has been seen in the perhaps similar case of city academies, big donations are few and far between. When they can be found, they often bring problems. The LSE's difficulties with support from Libya, or Imperial College's unfortunate experience with Gary Tanaka, are not attractive precedents.

If turning business schools into for-profits is the objective, how do we get there? The government does not own universities, and cannot force them to divest themselves of their business schools. It can, however, use its leverage to make this an attractive proposition for universities, by emphasising that they can keep the proceeds of the sale of schools or parts of schools either to outside businesses or through buy-outs or whatever other form entrepreneurs come up with. It can clarify or amend the legal position of universities and their component parts to give them greater freedom from European tendering requirements and other restrictive regulations.

The government can emphasise that this is the way it wants the sector to develop, and that there will be no further government funding for business schools. It can encourage other businesses to invest in the sector, perhaps initially as partners rather than as full beneficial owners, and it can make new entry easier – by, for example, fast-tracking applications from commercial providers to receive degree-awarding powers. It could also step up the competitive pressure by allowing British business students to use UK student loans (assuming these continue) to fund study at more private for-profits, overseas universities operating in the UK, or at universities abroad.

In the short run, it can put pressure on schools to become more cost-effective, and encourage existing private providers to expand provision, by reserving a proportion of student numbers for lower-cost providers that will charge lower fees, as David Willetts has begun to do. This is not a sustainable long-run position; rather it is a short-term expedient as a result of the coalition government's unwise move to reject the Browne Review's proposals on fees. But it indicates that the government is serious about the direction in which it would like this part of the sector to move.

All this may seem like political dynamite at the moment. But higher education in the UK has been through many changes in recent years and the boundaries of what is possible have expanded considerably. Despite good intentions, the sector is currently an expensive mess. Business schools have potentially got a way out of this mess into a brighter future which will benefit the schools, students, employers and the wider economy. If they have the courage to take this opportunity they may also offer lessons to the university sector as a whole.

References

Bennis, W. G. and J. O'Toole (2005), 'How business schools lost their way', *Harvard Business Review*, May.

Cooke, A. and V. Galt (2010), *The Impact of Business Schools in the UK*, Nottingham: Nottingham Business School and Association of Business Schools.

Davies, J. and H. Thomas (2009), 'What do business school deans do? Insights from a UK study', *Management Decision*, 47(9): 1396–1419.

Department for Business Innovation and Skills (2009), *Higher Ambitions: The future of universities in a knowledge economy*, London: BIS.

Dolton, P. and G. Makepeace (2011), 'Public and private sector labour markets', in P. Gregg and J. Wadsworth (eds), *The Labour Market in Winter*, Oxford: Oxford University Press.

Griffiths, B. and H. Murray (1985), *Whose Business? A Radical Proposal to Privatise British Business Schools*, Hobart Paper 102, London: Institute of Economic Affairs.

Ivory, C., P. Miskell, H. Shipton, A. White, K. Moeslin and A. Neely (2006), *UK Business Schools: Historical Contexts and Future Scenarios*, Advanced Institute of Management Research.

Khurana, R. (2007), *From Higher Aims to Hired Hands: The Social Transformation of American Business Schools and the Unfulfilled Promise of Management as a Profession*, Princeton, NJ: Princeton University Press.

Matthews, D. (2011), 'Business schools object to scale of cross-subsidisation', *Times Higher Education*, www.timeshighereducation.co.uk/story.asp?sectioncode=26&storycode=417626

Middlehurst, R. and J. Fielden (2011), *Private Providers in UK Higher Education: Some Policy Options*, Oxford: Higher Education Policy Institute.

Robinson, V. (2010), *How Do UK Business Schools Maintain Loyalty amongst Undergraduates? A Relationship-based Approach*, London: Association of Business Schools

Sastry, T. and B. Bekhradnia (2007), *The Academic Experience of Students in English Universities*, Oxford: Higher Education Policy Institute.

Shackleton, J. R. (2003), 'Opening up trade in higher education: a role for GATS?', *World Economics*, 4(4): 55–77.

Shephard, N. (2010), 'Deferred fees for universities', *Economic Affairs*, 30(2): 40–44.

Stanfield, J. (2009), *The Broken University*, London: Adam Smith Institute.

Taylor, C. (2009), *How English Universities Could Learn from the American Higher Education System*, IEA Discussion Paper 25, London: Institute of Economic Affairs.

Times Higher Education (2010), 'David Willetts acts on pledge to boost private providers', www.timeshighereducation.co.uk/story.asp?storycode=412737

Universities UK (2010), *The growth of private and for-profit higher education providers in the UK*, London: Universities UK.

Williams, A. O. P. (2010), *The History of UK Business and Management Education*, Bingley: Emerald.

10 CUSTOMISED SCHOOLING AND ENTREPRENEURSHIP IN THE USA

Frederick M. Hess

In an era when technology and cultural norms have made radical customisation the rule in everything from cell phones to web browsers, it is notable that the vast majority of school reforms are 'system-wide' measures that do little to bend schools into a shape more suitable for serving students with diverse needs. Indeed, many of those who argue in favour of increasing accountability, merit pay and school choice have often emphasised 'whole school' assumptions that simply presume traditional schools and classrooms as given. Such a mindset is ultimately crippling, because it ties us to an antiquated, bureaucratic system that neglects individual needs and limits access to high-quality supplemental instruction to the affluent families who can afford to buy it.

The problem with the 'whole school' assumption

Twenty-first-century school reformers have inherited a model of state education that dates from the early twentieth century and was born of an era marked by lurching, bureaucratic, black-box provision. This model is antithetical to specialisation and an awkward fit for a world where technology and tools have made it possible for new providers to deliver high-quality services that can be customised to targeted children or educators. Ironically, outside schools, children embrace such new technology with alacrity.

The reliance on this traditional whole school approach has impeded opportunities for innovation. In education, outside those providers who sell directly to affluent families, ventures offering online tutoring, language instruction, arts classes and much else are dependent upon their ability to convince district or school administrators that their service is useful. This is why many of the most dynamic providers of online education, such as SMARTHINKING and Tutor.com, are in higher education, selling directly to families, or selling to libraries and the US Department of Education; only rarely do they sell to schools. The result is perverse, trapping educators and students in a ghetto where powerful new tools and services are curiosities rather than routine parts of the school day.

What does 'unbundling' mean?

Becoming comfortable with customised schooling options first requires unbundling familiar notions of what is meant by education, shifting the conversation from 'school' to 'schooling', from 'teacher' to 'teaching'. If we reimagine schools as mechanisms that provide students with an assortment of services instead of delivering an indivisible package of 'education', we can start to disentangle the components of that package and customise them to fit specific student needs and abilities. Harnessing new technologies and crafting policies that support such customisation are vital steps to successfully upending our familiar approaches to delivering education.

There are two dimensions along which we can think about

unbundling. The first is structural unbundling, in which we think in new ways about what it means to be a 'teacher', a 'school' or a 'school system' and explore the ways in which we can rethink how schooling is delivered. The second dimension is content unbundling, or the unbundling of the 'stuff' of learning, in which we revisit assumptions about the scope and sequence of what students are taught and what they are expected to learn, thereby enabling the emergence of new, more varied approaches to curriculum and coursework.

The goal for customised, unbundled school reform is not to develop a new model of what a good school should look like but to cultivate a flexible system that emphasises performance, rewards success, addresses failure, and enables schools and a variety of specialised private providers to meet a variety of needs in increasingly effective and targeted ways.

Technology and the rise of virtual schooling

If we are to rethink the one-teacher-to-25-students classroom that has persisted so stubbornly for centuries, we must learn to exploit strategically the power of new technologies. As has been noted by Clayton Christensen et al. (2008) and by Chubb and Moe (2009), technology can facilitate customisation of coursework driven by real-time, sophisticated assessments; a freeing of education from the constraints of location; a deeper engagement of parents and teachers in their students' progress; and a more efficient means for educating more children with lower costs.

These have penetrated in some areas of the USA. Virtual schooling, in which students participate in schooling via online forums, video chats and other computer-based means, is used in Florida. Indeed, students in Florida have the right to choose Florida Virtual School (FLVS) as an educational option, and it currently serves 97,000 students who can enrol full- or part-time, throughout the year. Students study at their own pace and FLVS receives payment only once a student successfully completes a course. While the courses are free to Florida residents, students living outside of Florida and the USA are charged $375 per class per semester, and these courses are run by the school's for-profit arm, the FLVS Global School. School districts across the USA can also open a franchise virtual school making full use of FLVS courses, student support, teacher training and data management services. If the aim is to ensure that technology helps to promote customisation, and that today's new technologies do not become merely one more innovation layered on top of the familiar school model, it is necessary to update our notions of policy and accountability to fit the new era of schooling. Technological advances now make it possible for schooling to move past the one-size-fits-all model and more nimbly address discrete needs, but doing this at scale requires high-quality assessments that allow families to make good choices and which provide convincing public accountability.

Creating an entrepreneurial environment

Often products that will allow for customised learning come from outside the education sector. For-profit education would give schools incentives to take advantage of expertise outside the education sector and leverage those skills to provide services at a much lower cost than developing such expertise on their own. For education tools to be successful in signalling quality and thus stimulating demand among consumers, parents must know about them, know that they have a reputation for being high quality, and be able to choose those providers who use them. By creating a brand identity, toolmakers can better communicate their benefits to families and thus bolster the market with a greater awareness of quality providers.

The entrepreneurial promise is its capacity to unearth a Michael Dell or Bill Gates, and to benefit tens or hundreds of millions of people by encouraging these pioneers to build large-scale organisations that make high-quality, affordable home computers or software available to all. But existing institutions do not wish to contemplate 'risky' alternatives when dealing with children – they prefer solutions that minimise risk. This inspires calls for smaller classes, best practices, scientifically based research, more discipline and other seemingly 'risk-free' solutions. Discomfiture with entrepreneurial activity in education is due in part to how rarely our assumptions about reform are informed by frank consideration of how progress unfolds in other sectors. New solutions are going to be untested and are going to emerge through trial and error. As a result, entrepreneurship rejects the notion that we can somehow anticipate the future and then race there in an orderly fashion.

In education, even leaders heralded for their entrepreneurial bent tend to identify existing practice and replicate it while impeding new providers and hindering the next generation of problem-solvers. For example, while the US Knowledge is Power Program (KIPP) Academies have accumulated an impressive track record and national recognition, those involved are the first to acknowledge that their greatest triumph is proficiently executing a traditional model of schooling. They have succeeded by relentlessly focusing on results, recruiting talented educators, and forging a culture of commitment and hard work – rather than devising a fundamentally more productive model of schooling. KIPP deserves its accolades, but it should be celebrated as a glimmering of what an entrepreneurial environment makes possible – not the culmination of that process.

Rather than determining what schooling 'should' look like in the future, the entrepreneurial presumption seeks a flexible system that welcomes talent, focuses on results, rewards success, removes failures, and does not stifle the emergence of better solutions. The system must therefore move from one designed around inputs and institutional needs to one which is designed around individuals and results. Five essential principles should guide the design of such a system.

Five essential principles

Firstly, today's funding arrangements discourage creative problem-solving, the emergence of niche providers, and the search for new efficiencies. In the USA, state and federal regulations require nearly every district to provide similar bundles of services, while districts rarely use specialised providers to improve performance when it comes to services such as human resources, facilities or remedial instruction. The breaking of the stranglehold of the whole school model ultimately requires that states and districts shift away from a vision of choice in which students merely choose between schools and towards a model more akin to that of the 'health savings account' in healthcare. Rather than just paying for students to go to school A or B, the state would deposit dollars in a virtual account in the name of each student and then allow parents to use those dollars to allocate the funds to procure services from a variety of providers. Education finance should therefore be configured to accommodate non-profit and for-profit providers of niche instructional services and to reward cost-effective performance. Such a system would give families cause to start paying attention to the cost of services, would enable families to happily continue to use a local school but obtain certain programmes from elsewhere, and would permit approved providers to serve families directly without necessarily having to negotiate school district bureaucracies.

Secondly, this system must be dynamic and responsive. This requires the dissolution of familiar monopolies and the removal of barriers that stand in the way of new providers. Barriers to entry are the laws, rules and practices that make it harder or more costly to launch a new venture. Such barriers include: regulations hindering the opening of charter schools and regulations which restrict their ability to hire non-traditional teachers; state financing systems which fund charter schools at lower levels than traditional district schools; and textbook approval systems so onerous that only the largest publishers can successfully compete. Barriers worth particular attention are those that inhibit the opening of new schools or impose restraints on how new providers can operate.

Thirdly, a healthy entrepreneurial environment is transparent, with clear accountability for learning, service provision and financial practices. It requires readily available data on student learning and various other performance considerations (from procurement to maintenance to hiring) and compels providers to compete on both quality and cost. An example of the private sector meeting the need for data is the development of consumer review websites such as Schooldigger.com and GreatSchools.org, which provide searching parents with quick school data that make it easy to compare and choose from a number of options. Meanwhile, providers must also have reliable information on the needs and characteristics of those they will be serving.

Fourthly, the system should strive to attract a mass of talented and energetic individuals, retain and cultivate promising problem-solvers, and develop an infrastructure to support their efforts. Today, licensing requirements are among the factors that deter people from entering education. Hiring practices in many large districts in the USA are painfully slow, which alienates attractive candidates. Inflexible compensation systems penalise mobile workers, do little to reward top performers and provide expansive benefits that are most attractive to those who stay in place for decades. Measures to produce a more entrepreneur-friendly environment include loosening certification barriers and basing compensation on performance rather than on seniority.

Finally, schooling must move decisively away from a system governed by inputs and regulation to one ordered around individuals and results. This requires recognising students' varying needs and conceding that education is not a one-size-fits-all enterprise.

Nothing ventured, nothing gained

New ventures can neither launch nor grow without money. There are three general sources that can be tapped to support educational start-ups: profit-seeking investors, non-profit associations, and public agencies.

For-profit investment in education has been rare because capital typically flows to ventures that offer an attractive, risk-adjusted return, which has generally not existed in schooling.

But there are steps that would help the sector attract more private funding to support research, development and creative problem-solving. For instance, clear standards for judging effectiveness can reassure investors that ventures will be less subject to political influence and better positioned to succeed if demonstrably effective. Entrepreneur-friendly reform is also undermined directly by statutes that restrict the involvement of for-profit firms in school management.

Given the dearth of private investment and the constrained nature of public spending, entrepreneurial ventures to date have been disproportionately funded by the tiny sliver of money that philanthropies contribute – especially funds from younger foundations with roots in the new economy. Traditionally, foundations have sought to avoid controversy, pay attention to professional direction, and foster consensus. Today, however, several of the most influential education philanthropies – including the Gates, Walton and Broad foundations – are consciously supporting riskier, less conventional endeavours. Perhaps the most interesting example is the NewSchools Venture Fund, a 'venture philanthropy' that secures investments from third parties and then seeks to provide start-up capital to scalable, sustainable breakthrough ventures – both non-profit and for-profit.

In the end, if the introduction of entrepreneurship in education is to be successful, we must accept that it is possible to educate children in radically more effective ways. The acceptance of entrepreneurship will mean, however, that some ventures will fail in order to avoid a larger risk – persistent mediocrity. But the risk of failure means that efforts to cultivate supply-side reform must be coupled with attention to devising new, more nimble systems of knowledge creation and quality control that can help education leaders, policymakers and entrepreneurs negotiate the challenges of modern school reform.

The greatest educational risk we confront today lies not in embracing entrepreneurship but in continuing to cling to an inadequate and increasingly anachronistic status quo. The failed ideas, providers and schools produced by entrepreneurial activity may be a high price to pay. But it is a price worth paying to avoid the stagnation and ceaseless tinkering that have for so long been the face of school reform.

Conclusion

It is clear that choice-based reformers have previously placed too much faith in the presumption that simply permitting families to choose their child's school will foster a dynamic sector. Choice is only half of the supply-and-demand market equation. Proposals that increase parental choice may boost demand but typically do not address the supply of good-quality options. For decades, school-choice reformers have worked to increase choice only among schools, thereby missing an opportunity to appeal to those parents who may not be willing to change schools, but would be interested in greater choice among tutors, lesson plans or instructional approaches.

Instead of focusing on isolated strategies to fix schools or promote choice, supply-side reforms focus on making the ecosystem more hospitable to the emergence and expansion of effective problem-solvers. Such an approach focuses on creating conditions that enable problem-solvers and does not presume that elected officials, district leaders, professors or funders can systematically identify and implement workable solutions that are known in advance. Radical and disruptive improvement results from new entrants creating a product or formula that works and devising an organisation and culture that provide for fidelity to the innovation at increasing scale. This is why no generation of schools or educational providers should ever be regarded as the ultimate solution. The aim should be to facilitate a dynamic sector in which this self-replenishing process becomes the norm.

Conventional schools represent best-practice solutions of an earlier age – indeed, they developed in the USA and the UK when the profit motive was allowed. Today, however, heightened aspirations, changing student needs and the opportunities presented by new tools and technologies mean that old arrangements must be challenged by competition. We need greater educational choice, not just school choice.

References

Christensen, C., M. Horn and C. Johnson (2008), *Disrupting Class: How Disruptive Innovation Will Change the Way the World Learns*, New York: McGraw-Hill.

Chubb, J. and T. Moe (2009), *Liberating Learning: Technology, Politics, and the Future of American Education*, San Francisco: Jossey Bass.

11 PRIVATE CAPITAL, FOR-PROFIT ENTERPRISES AND PUBLIC EDUCATION

Tom Vander Ark

Education remains one of the few sectors that information and communication technologies have not transformed. There has been very little productivity improvement in US schools, despite a doubling of per-pupil funding over the past two decades. While the government delivery system is inflexible and bureaucratic and provides an inadequate impetus for performance and improvement, non-profit organisations have limited ability to aggregate capital for research and development or scaled impact. While non-profits often chase the interest of foundations, they lack the funding to develop their operating infrastructure and leadership. Other than passion for their mission, non-profit managers have weak incentives for growth and performance. In contrast, for-profit enterprises may have greater ability to attract talent and capital, greater incentives to achieve scaled impact, and the ability to use multiple business strategies. In the private sector, managers have incentives, including share-price-related and performance compensation that encourage quality, performance and growth. Private investment will not fix the problems with education, but education will not be fixed without it.

Private capital and for-profit enterprises will therefore play a vital role in creating tools that increase the productivity of learning, staffing and facilities; develop formats and services that leverage these tools; manage high-quality, cost-effective education networks; and lead the sector transition from batch processing – in which learning is organised around classes of students of the same age, who progress through material at the same pace – to personalised, digital learning services.

Batch-print to personal digital learning services

The barriers of a state delivery system in education have inhibited the flow of private capital. Diffused and protracted procurement systems, reluctance on the part of those who administer schools to work with for-profit companies and the resulting weak returns on investment have made investment in the US education sector unusually low. Schools, particularly in the USA, are giant, expensive facilities that sit empty about half the time, often unused on evenings and weekends. School budgets are driven by staffing ratios that, unlike in most other sectors, have not changed with productivity-improving technology. Young people learn about the same amount and at about the same speed that they did one hundred years ago.

The opportunity to learn more, faster, and cheaper, however, is now becoming a reality. To the extent that delivery systems embrace market opportunities, investment in new learning tools and new school formats, they will yield improved productivity and make worldwide access to high-quality, cost-effective learning experiences possible. The waves of innovation in other sectors outline the productivity revolution to come.

By 2020, the majority of students in developed countries will do the majority of their learning online. Schools will look more like a Starbucks, where young people attend at convenient times and where their learning extends into the community. Low-cost formats that blend online and onsite learning will make it more cost-effective for low-income communities to have access to high-quality secondary education. These advances will reshape how material is delivered, how teachers interact with one another, how students are assessed, and the basic concept of the classroom and the teaching profession.

Students will learn by engaging virtual worlds with continual background assessment of their skills and interests. A well-constructed online learning process is easy to enter and hard to master; each player rides a learning curve through engaging content with tools and roles that evolve to meet new challenges. Early entrants in the online learning space include Tabula Digita's Dimension M, a maths game, and in the informal space, Grockit, a two-dimensional quiz bowl for students preparing for the Graduate Management Admission Test (GMAT).

Most schools will adopt voluntary national standards with fewer, clearer and higher learning objectives and sophisticated online assessments that quickly focus on a student's learning level. Built into many learning experiences, these adaptive assessments will provide continual performance feedback to students, teachers and content developers. Expert systems will queue content, provide support, make connections and suggest learning pathways while managing a personal, portable learning profile. Delivery will work seamlessly across a variety of inexpensive personal digital devices.

With powerful new resources online, home schooling (including students in virtual charter schools) will double in size in the USA, exceeding 10 per cent of all students. Given the continuing interest in ensuring that children are looked after during the day and in extra-curricular activities, however, the vast majority of students will learn in hybrid environments that blend online and onsite learning in smart, agile schools. Some of these hybrid environments will demonstrate significant productivity gains in learning, staffing and facilities. Students will attend during convenient times of the day and year, reducing the rigid effects of the agrarian calendar that still determines school holidays. Well-paid teachers and flexible spaces will serve larger numbers of students at lower cost. In the developing world, hybrid formats and inexpensive devices will extend access to high-quality, low-cost secondary education.

New openings for private capital

The inefficiency of the US state schooling system has hampered investment and innovation. Purchasing is done by 15,000 districts and more than 100,000 schools, leading to diffused and protracted sales efforts. A web of interlocking employment agreements and local policies is compounded by 50 different complex education codes that deter interest from the private sector. The combination of a decentralised system, subtle and outright barriers to entry and tight budgets has dampened private investment. Vendors of new learning and educational management products and services find it difficult to find entry points and grow profitably. US state schooling spending is in excess of $600 billion and the for-profit market is around $25 billion. The latter has three large segments: instructional materials; technology infrastructure; and related services, including tutoring, professional development and school improvement. The following five emerging areas are slowly opening the sector to additional investment and innovation.

Inexpensive application development

Flexible social networking applications such as Facebook and Ning.com allow easy group formation and customisation. The addition of game elements in Grockit.com provides a fun and useful place for GMAT students to study together. Applications that would not have been possible or would have been very expensive can now be rapidly and inexpensively prototyped.

Online learning

The segment continues to grow by more than 30 per cent annually – more than 50 per cent where policies encourage participation – with a growing number of government and private participants. Blended learning – learning while online in a classroom – is the fastest-growing segment. The *Digital Learning Now*[1] report is a blueprint for the blended learning future and recommends that all students should be able to customise their education using digital content through an approved provider. More specifically, it recommends that states: allow students to take online classes full-time, part-time or by individual course; allow students to enrol with multiple providers and blend online courses with onsite learning; allow rolling enrolment all year round; do not limit the number of credits earned online; and, finally, do not limit provider options for delivering instruction. The emerging vision for education is school as a service: open your browser and you have learning options, multiple providers, multiple devices, customised engaging learning anywhere, any time.

1 Published by the Foundation for Excellence in Education, December 2010.

Open content

While most open educational resources (OERs) are a product of government effort and foundation investment, the Redhat/Linux model of a robust service economy around open content is emerging in education. Wireless Generation, a Brooklyn start-up, purchased a reading textbook, put it online, and gave it away free of charge at FreeReading.net. Wireless Generation earns money from FreeReading.net by selling aligned assessment, professional development and customised content delivery. In an exciting development, other entrepreneurial for-profit and non-profit partners have expanded the array of related services. This micro-economy around a free reading text is a small example of the substantial OER vendor community that will develop in the coming decade, along with organised, vetted and comprehensive OER libraries.

Educational services

Direct-to-consumer services, both for formal credit accumulation and informal personal development, are set to be the next wave of innovation. Numerous online tutoring services such as Tutor.com, e-Tutor.com, etutorworld, Smarthinking and Eduxcel.com have been introduced, together with several sophisticated adaptive learning games such as Dreambox.com. Although education is a decade behind the gaming sector, adaptive secondary maths curricula such as Carnegie Learning and Reasoning Mind are promising; adaptive learning games MangaHigh and Dimension M are gaining viral adoption; and adaptive primary maths products such as Dreambox which power the high-performing Rocketship network are also promising. In addition, Quest to

Learn is a new game-based school in New York City with an enquiry-based modular curriculum which incorporates game-play dynamics into the learning experience.

School operations

After a disappointing introduction with Edison, for-profit school operators have quietly emerged as a multi-billion-dollar subsector. Like open content, this trend follows successful introduction at the post-secondary level with a number of scaled participants operating online and onsite programmes including Apollo (University of Phoenix), DeVry, Strayer, Capella and Corinthian. For-profit education management organisations such as National Heritage Academies, Mosaica and Leona are now collectively larger than non-profit charter management organisations, with over $1 billion in combined revenue. For-profit private school networks such as Meritas and American Education Group are acquiring individual schools and building substantial networks. Online learning providers K12 Inc. and KC Distance Learning Inc. are rapidly expanding through virtual charter schools and are increasingly reaching into classrooms in government schools by offering credit recovery for students that are behind and academic acceleration opportunities for advanced students.

There is some government activity in these five areas, but it is private investment which is pushing these frontiers as the sector shifts from batch-print to digital personal learning services. These areas represent new entry points and business models for private capital.

The innovation agenda

The growth of media and communications technology, the rise of a new generation of students and teachers equipped to use technology and the shifts within schools and education systems themselves create new fertile ground for education innovation.

One emerging capability that is helping to meet the challenge is the rich informal learning ecosystem (Wikipedia, search, peer-to-peer, Khan Academy, and so on) that is surrounding the formal education system. Schools that blend the best of online learning and onsite support have the potential to customise learning for every student, to boost motivation and double the academic time spent on a task – and do it without spending more money. Indeed, children are already blending their own education by taking online courses where states allow it.

With the explosion of instructional content, it is becoming easier for students to choose the most effective mode of instruction for them: recorded tutorials (KhanAcademy.org), live tutoring (Tutor.com), short videos (BrightStorm.com), games (Funbrain.com), lectures (AcademicEarth.com), text with voice-over (Hippocampus.org), and Flexbooks for e-readers (CK12.org) are all available. Soon there will be several platforms with smart engines that, like School of One, recommend the right lesson in the right mode at the right time. They will build smart mixed-mode playlists that will eventually include more than skill-building exercises. Second-generation playlists will include integration, application and extension opportunities.

As personal digital learning platforms mature, enabling a rapid expansion of schools that focus on students and learning and not instructors and classes, students in high school and college will increasingly be allowed to chart their own pathways, assembling a personal transcript from multiple providers. Their ultimate formal certification may be place-based, but their education will be unbounded.

Progress of the sort outlined above will depend on the reduction of government-imposed barriers and the introduction of incentives for innovation. The shift from batch-print to personalised digital services will accelerate the transition to these kinds of contract operations. This transition is likely to be bumpy and uneven across political boundaries. States and cities open to innovation will see a rapid increase in learning options – virtual and blended schools, branded networks and new configurations that include high-school and post-secondary certificates. Federal, state and local governments, in partnership with non-governmental organisations and charities, will play an important role in expanding access to quality learning by investing in research and development and by improving incentives for entrepreneurs. Perhaps the most important government role, however, will be to create the policy room to allow innovation.

The for-profit advantage

The private sector will play the critical role in educational innovation given its unique ability to aggregate capital around disruptive ideas, hire talented teams and invest in multi-channel marketing. These three factors offer distinct advantages compared with non-profits. Firstly, while it is not easy to raise angel and early-stage venture capital, it is often easier than raising unrestricted grant funding. Secondly, the ability to offer shares and share options to founders and early team members makes it easier to attract world-class talent to for-profit enterprises. Finally, the ability to execute a multi-channel strategy – including targeting lucrative markets (such as high-income customers) rather than exclusively low-income students and serving a charitable purpose – can make for-profit business models easier to fund and scale. Indeed, a for-profit service that reaches 10 million students is likely to serve a larger number of low-income students than a non-profit designed specifically for the purpose of reaching low-income students.

Compared with the non-profit and state sectors, private investment in for-profit ventures has significant advantages in achieving quality at scale. State schools are organised for compliance and employee protection rather than performance and have little incentive to scale successful models. Non-profits have difficulty raising capital to operate at scale and lack incentives to scale successful ideas. In contrast, for-profit organisations have strong incentives to satisfy customers and achieve scale and are playing an important scaling role with regard to learning tools, schools and services.

The growing role of for-profit enterprise in education parallels the growth of the internet, which has expanded access to learning opportunities worldwide. Integration of distance learning and face-to-face courses has increased access to post-secondary learning, improved student performance and reduced costs. Nearly two-thirds of undergraduate degree programmes in the USA offer web-based courses with a growing number, especially of private for-profit universities, offering entire degrees online. Meanwhile, China now has more students engaged in post-secondary education than the USA, and it is clear that it will not be able to support the shift from elite to mass higher education without embracing online learning and private providers.

Combining philanthropy and profit-seeking investment

The recent increase in the number of young software billionaires in the USA has been accompanied by a dramatic increase in education philanthropy that is oriented more towards new ventures and is less bounded by the roles and rules of traditional charity. Philanthropic investors are increasingly pressing non-profits to think like for-profits and develop a sustainable business model and scaled solutions.

A number of organisations already blend philanthropic grants and profit-seeking investments to achieve strategic impact objectives. Examples include Google.org, Omidyar Network and the New School Venture Fund. These initiatives are not limited to education. There are a growing number of examples from the global health sector that blend philanthropic and profit-seeking capital, including the Clinton Global Initiative's effort mitigating market risk for pharmaceutical giant GSK by aggregating demand for HIV treatment drugs.

The shift from batch-print education to digital personal learning services will require coordinated impact capital, both philanthropic and venture capital. In the future we will see more examples of this blended capital. This might include the development of for-profit financial services for charter schools with philanthropic credit guarantees or an investment in for-profit private school operations in voucher cities and states that provide incentives for serving low-income students or taking over failed state schools.

The backlash and beyond

Primary and, to a slightly lesser extent, secondary education is increasingly viewed globally – rightly or wrongly – as a public good and a civil right. In most countries, private schools augment government delivery, and profit-seeking textbook, school supplies and business service vendors are widely accepted as an integral part of the delivery systems for state schools. There are many who believe, however, that profit-seeking companies cross the line when they propose to take on operational responsibility for schools. Some seem to find the thought of taxation receipts producing a return to shareholders in exchange for educational services simply offensive, despite similar arrangements with road contractors, hospital operators or private prisons. US society has also accepted a diverse post-secondary market subsidised with government scholarships, but remains cautious about the private operation of primary and secondary schools.

Private investment in for-profit enterprises will be critical to expanding global access to quality education by producing and scaling innovative learning tools and formats. Hybrid formats that blend online learning with onsite support also have the potential to deliver low-cost, high-quality secondary education worldwide. Government policy and investment can accelerate the contributions of the private sector by creating incentives for software developers and school operators. Policies that will maximise private investment include vouchers or private school scholarships that allow low-income students full school choice, and incentives for organisations, including for-profit operators, to take over or replace failing government schools

There will certainly be unscrupulous organisations that try to profit from government grants while not providing high-quality education, but the same is true in many other areas of government policy. With adequate monitoring and thoughtful contracting, for-profit organisations can leverage government investment in educational research and development spending and will undoubtedly produce critical innovations in learning tools and formats.

The revolution is moving much faster than previously thought. According to Ambient Insight, more than four million US students are learning online; e-learning is growing by 46 per cent annually; and more than one third of US students will be doing at least a portion of their learning online by 2015. I am convinced that at least two-thirds of US students will be learning online by the end of the decade. This has important implications. Instead of fighting old reform battles, we should focus on shaping the shift to personal digital learning. Reformulating old debates can result in win-win-win solutions for students, teachers and parents.

ABOUT THE IEA

The Institute is a research and educational charity (No. CC 235 351), limited by guarantee. Its mission is to improve understanding of the fundamental institutions of a free society by analysing and expounding the role of markets in solving economic and social problems.

The IEA achieves its mission by:

- a high-quality publishing programme
- conferences, seminars, lectures and other events
- outreach to school and college students
- brokering media introductions and appearances

The IEA, which was established in 1955 by the late Sir Antony Fisher, is an educational charity, not a political organisation. It is independent of any political party or group and does not carry on activities intended to affect support for any political party or candidate in any election or referendum, or at any other time. It is financed by sales of publications, conference fees and voluntary donations.

In addition to its main series of publications the IEA also publishes a termly journal, *Economic Affairs*.

The IEA is aided in its work by a distinguished international Academic Advisory Council and an eminent panel of Honorary Fellows. Together with other academics, they review prospective IEA publications, their comments being passed on anonymously to authors. All IEA papers are therefore subject to the same rigorous independent refereeing process as used by leading academic journals.

IEA publications enjoy widespread classroom use and course adoptions in schools and universities. They are also sold throughout the world and often translated/reprinted.

Since 1974 the IEA has helped to create a worldwide network of 100 similar institutions in over 70 countries. They are all independent but share the IEA's mission.

Views expressed in the IEA's publications are those of the authors, not those of the Institute (which has no corporate view), its Managing Trustees, Academic Advisory Council members or senior staff.

Members of the Institute's Academic Advisory Council, Honorary Fellows, Trustees and Staff are listed on the following page.

The Institute gratefully acknowledges financial support for its publications programme and other work from a generous benefaction by the late Alec and Beryl Warren.

The Institute of Economic Affairs
2 Lord North Street, Westminster, London SW1P 3LB
Tel: 020 7799 8900
Fax: 020 7799 2137
Email: iea@iea.org.uk
Internet: iea.org.uk

Other papers recently published by the IEA include:

Taxation and Red Tape
The Cost to British Business of Complying with the UK Tax System
Francis Chittenden, Hilary Foster & Brian Sloan
Research Monograph 64; ISBN 978 0 255 36612 0; £12.50

Ludwig von Mises – A Primer
Eamonn Butler
Occasional Paper 143; ISBN 978 0 255 36629 8; £7.50

Does Britain Need a Financial Regulator?
Statutory Regulation, Private Regulation and Financial Markets
Terry Arthur & Philip Booth
Hobart Paper 169; ISBN 978 0 255 36593 2; £12.50

Hayek's *The Constitution of Liberty*
An Account of Its Argument
Eugene F. Miller
Occasional Paper 144; ISBN 978 0 255 36637 3; £12.50

Fair Trade Without the Froth
A Dispassionate Economic Analysis of 'Fair Trade'
Sushil Mohan
Hobart Paper 170; ISBN 978 0 255 36645 8; £10.00

A New Understanding of Poverty
Poverty Measurement and Policy Implications
Kristian Niemietz
Research Monograph 65; ISBN 978 0 255 36638 0; £12.50

The Challenge of Immigration
A Radical Solution
Gary S. Becker
Occasional Paper 145; ISBN 978 0 255 36613 7; £7.50

Sharper Axes, Lower Taxes
Big Steps to a Smaller State
Edited by Philip Booth
Hobart Paperback 38; ISBN 978 0 255 36648 9; £12.50

Self-employment, Small Firms and Enterprise
Peter Urwin
Research Monograph 66; ISBN 978 0 255 36610 6; £12.50

Crises of Governments
The Ongoing Global Financial Crisis and Recession
Robert Barro
Occasional Paper 146; ISBN 978 0 255 36657 1; £7.50

... and the Pursuit of Happiness
Wellbeing and the Role of Government
Edited by Philip Booth
Readings 64; ISBN 978 0 255 36656 4; £12.50

Public Choice – A Primer
Eamonn Butler
Occasional Paper 147; ISBN 978 0 255 36650 2; £10.00

Other IEA publications

Comprehensive information on other publications and the wider work of the IEA can be found at www.iea.org.uk. To order any publication please see below.

Personal customers

Orders from personal customers should be directed to the IEA:

Clare Rusbridge
IEA
2 Lord North Street
FREEPOST LON10168
London SW1P 3YZ
Tel: 020 7799 8907. Fax: 020 7799 2137
Email: crusbridge@iea.org.uk

Trade customers

All orders from the book trade should be directed to the IEA's distributor:

Gazelle Book Services Ltd (IEA Orders)
FREEPOST RLYS-EAHU-YSCZ
White Cross Mills
Hightown
Lancaster LA1 4XS
Tel: 01524 68765. Fax: 01524 53232
Email: sales@gazellebooks.co.uk

IEA subscriptions

The IEA also offers a subscription service to its publications. For a single annual payment (currently £42.00 in the UK), subscribers receive every monograph the IEA publishes. For more information please contact:

Clare Rusbridge
Subscriptions
IEA
2 Lord North Street
FREEPOST LON10168
London SW1P 3YZ
Tel: 020 7799 8907. Fax: 020 7799 2137
Email: crusbridge@iea.org.uk